Human-Computer Interaction Series

HCI is a multidisciplinary field focused on human aspects of the development of computer technology. As computer-based technology becomes increasingly pervasive—not just in developed countries, but worldwide—the need to take a human-centered approach in the design and development of this technology becomes ever more important. For roughly 30 years now, researchers and practitioners in computational and behavioral sciences have worked to identify theory and practice that influences the direction of these technologies, and this diverse work makes up the field of human-computer interaction. Broadly speaking it includes the study of what technology might be able to do for people and how people might interact with the technology. The HCI series publishes books that advance the science and technology of developing systems which are both effective and satisfying for people in a wide variety of contexts. Titles focus on theoretical perspectives (such as formal approaches drawn from a variety of behavioral sciences), practical approaches (such as the techniques for effectively integrating user needs in system development), and social issues (such as the determinants of utility, usability and acceptability).

For further volumes:
http://www.springer.com/series/6033

Victor M.R. Penichet • Antonio Peñalver
José A. Gallud

Editors

New Trends in Interaction, Virtual Reality and Modeling

 Springer

Editors

Victor M.R. Penichet
Computing Systems Department
University of Castilla-La Mancha
Albacete
Spain

José A. Gallud
Computing Systems Department
University of Castilla-La Mancha
Albacete
Spain

Antonio Peñalver
Center of Operations Research
  University Institute
University of Elche
Elche, Alicante
Spain

ISSN 1571-5035
ISBN 978-1-4471-7239-0   ISBN 978-1-4471-5445-7 (eBook)
DOI 10.1007/978-1-4471-5445-7
Springer London Heidelberg New York Dordrecht

Printed on acid-free paper

Springer is part of Springer Science+Business Media (www.springer.com)

Preface

Human-Computer Interaction (HCI) is a research area in Computer Science concerned with the design, implementation, and evaluation of interactive systems, where the user is the key and the center of the process. Many disciplines are closely related to HCI: psychology, cognitive science, ergonomics, sociology, business, graphic design, collaboration, software engineering, and so forth. Its main objective relies on the study of human factors, current technology, and how the interaction between humans and such technologies may be accomplished in the most natural and easy way. The field of application is quite extensive since the purpose is not what to do but how to design it to suit the users' needs.

This volume, which forms part of Springer's Human-Computer Interaction Series, presents a selection of research articles focused on new trends in interaction, especially some issues regarding virtual and augmented reality, modeling, and evaluation. *New Trends in Interaction, Virtual Reality and Modeling* has been written as the result of the collaboration and the work of a number of researchers from many universities, research institutes, and companies. The selection of the chapters has been possible due to the joint conference between the HCI communities of Spain and Mexico, celebrated in October 2012. The International Conference Interacción 2012 was held at the Miguel Hernandez University of Elche (Spain) and the Mexican Conference MexIHC 2012 was held at the Instituto Tecnológico Autónomo de México (ITAM), Mexico, DF.

Interacción 2012 was the 13th edition of the International Conference promoted by the Spanish *Asociación para la Interacción Persona-Ordenador* (AIPO), whose main objective was to promote and disseminate the recent advances in the field of Human-Computer Interaction. It was organized by the research groups WEBDE-CISION and HCI&PR from the Center of Operations Research University Institute of the Miguel Hernandez University of Elche (UMH) and had the support of the ISE Research Group from the Albacete Research Institute of Informatics (I3A) at the University of Castilla-La Mancha (UCLM) and the Faculty of Computing and Information Technology at King Abdulaziz University (KAU).

MexIHC 2012 was the fourth Conference on Human-Computer Interaction, organized by the Mexican ACM SIGCHI chapter (CHI-México) in a biennial format alternating with the Latin American Conference on Human-Computer Interaction (CLIHC). It was organized by research professors and researchers from the HCI community in Mexico, members of Mexican institutions of higher education such as Instituto Tecnológico Autónomo de México (ITAM); Universidad Autónoma de Baja California (UABC); Universidad Autónoma Metropolitana Unidad Cuajimalpa (UAM-C); the Centro de Investigación Científica y de Educación Superior de Ensenada, Baja California (CICESE); and Universidad Tecnológica de la Mixteca (UTM).

Both conferences were celebrated jointly, keeping their own identities, to join forces and establish partnerships between the two communities.

The book has been organized in a set of ten short chapters to cover different application domains, as follows.

The first chapter, presents an agile method for exploiting desktop eye tracker equipment in combination with mobile devices. Then, Chap. 2, describes SV (Scheme Visualization) as an approach to explore large-scale collections based on classification systems. Chapter 3, introduces a framework based on the use of modeling and components composition techniques, which is intended to simplify the development of organizational collaborative systems. Chapter 4, presents a low-cost virtual reality system that provides highly satisfying virtual experiences. Chapter 5, introduces the most popular hardware and software tools and technologies to develop Augmented Reality (AR) and Mixed Reality (MR) applications, in order to serve as a starting point to anyone interested in developing such systems. Chapter 6, describes an implementation based on the Virtual Reality Peripheral Network to handle connectivity between Virtual Reality (VR) applications and SensAble® Technology Phantom Haptic Devices using the OpenHaptics 3.0 Haptic Library Application Programmable Interface (HLAPI). Chapter 7, presents the results of a research study implementing a teaching technological strategy to help children with Down syndrome develop their reading skills. Chapter 8, introduces several platform-independent models to overcome this problem by decreasing the level of cohesion between communication technologies and software for ubiquitous computing. Chapter 9, presents a method for applying gamification as a tool to improve the participation and motivation of people in performing different tasks. Finally, Chap. 10, describes a suite of five structural principles known as BaLOReS, together with five aesthetic metrics. These principles help designers to structure their mock-ups which are later assessed through the metrics.

We would like to thank all authors and people involved in the book for their time and effort. Special thanks to Helen Desmond (Springer Computer Science Editor) and the Springer team for giving us the opportunity to prepare this volume. We hope the reader finds this book informative and useful for both research and practice.

Victor M.R. Penichet
Antonio Peñalver
José A. Gallud

Contents

Contributors

Jorge Augusto Universidad Rey Juan Carlos, Madrid, Spain

Kawtar Benghazi ETSIIT, Department of Computer Languages and Systems, University of Granada, Granada, Spain

Antonio Benitez Ruiz Laboratorio de Percepción por Computadora, Universidad Politécnica de Puebla, Puebla, Mexico

Crescencio Bravo Santos Computer Science and Engineering Faculty, Department of Information Technologies and Systems, University of Castilla-La Mancha, Ciudad Real, Spain

Cira Cuadrat Seix GRIHO HCI Research Laboratory, University of Lleida, Spain

Maria Cuevas-Rodriguez Departamento de Tecnología Electrónica, Universidad de Málaga, Malaga, Spain

Jorge de la Calleja Mora Laboratorio de Percepción por Computadora, Universidad Politécnica de Puebla, Puebla, Mexico

Ernesto de La Rubia Department of Electronic Technology, University of Malaga, Malaga, Spain

Antonio Diaz-Estrella Department of Electronic Technology, University of Malaga, Malaga, Spain

Andrés Francisco-Aparicio GEDES Research Group, ETS de Ingeniería Informática, University of Granada, Granada, Spain

Jesús Gallardo Casero Polytechnic School of Teruel, Department of Information Technologies and Systems, University of Zaragoza, Teruel, Spain

José Antonio Gallud ESII, University of Castilla-La Mancha, Albacete, Spain

Pascual González López LoUISE Research Group, Computer System Department, University of Castilla-La Mancha, Albacete, Spain

Salvador González López LoUISE Research Group, Computer System Department, University of Castilla-La Mancha, Albacete, Spain

José Luis González Sánchez GEDES Research Group, ETS de Ingeniería Informática, University of Granada, Granada, Spain

Francisco Luis Gutiérrez-Vela GEDES Research Group, ETS de Ingeniería Informática, University of Granada, Granada, Spain

José Luis Isla-Montes Department of Computer Languages and Systems, Universidad de Cádiz, Cádiz, Spain

Sergio López Antonaya Computer Science and Engineering Faculty, Department of Information Technologies and Systems, University of Castilla-La Mancha, Ciudad Real, Spain

José Luis Garrido ETSIIT, Department of Computer Languages and Systems, University of Granada, Granada, Spain

María Auxilio Medina Nieto Laboratorio de Percepción por Computadora, Universidad Politécnica de Puebla, Puebla, Mexico

Luis Molina-Tanco Departamento de Tecnología Electrónica, Universidad de Málaga, Malaga, Spain

Francisco Montero Simarro LoUISE Research Group, Computer System Department, University of Castilla-La Mancha, Albacete, Spain

Bárbara Paola Muro Haro University of Colima, Colima, Mexico

Hector Olmedo Universidad de Valladolid, Valladolid, Spain

Universidad Rey Juan Carlos, Madrid, Spain

Antonio Peñalver Center of Operations Research University Institute, University of Elche, Elche, Alicante, Spain

Victor M.R. Penichet ESII, University of Castilla-La Mancha, Albacete, Spain

Matthieu Poyade Departamento de Tecnología Electrónica, Universidad de Málaga, Malaga, Spain

Arcadio Reyes-Lecuona Departamento de Tecnología Electrónica, Universidad de Málaga, Malaga, Spain

Carlos Rodríguez-Domínguez ETSIIT, Department of Computer Languages and Systems, University of Granada, Granada, Spain

Juan José Rodríguez Soler Gneis, Madrid, Spain

J. Alfredo Sánchez Human-Computer Interaction Laboratory, Universidad de las Américas – Puebla, Puebla, Mexico

Pedro Santana University of Colima, Colima, Mexico

Montserrat Sendín Veloso GRIHO HCI Research Laboratory, University of Lleida, Spain

Aurora Valenzuela Garach Faculty of Medicine, Department of Forensic Medicine, Toxicology and Physical Anthropology, University of Granada, Granada, Spain

Chapter 1
Validating a Method for Quantitative Mobile Usability Testing Based on Desktop Eyetracking

Montserrat Sendín Veloso, Juan José Rodríguez Soler, and Cira Cuadrat Seix

Abstract With the fast evolution in the development of applications for mobile devices, the study and adequacy of usability evaluation methodologies in this context is increasingly in demand. Current equipment particularly adapted to these types of interfaces, such as specific eyetracking equipment for mobile devices, is trying to offer a solution to contexts related to mobility. However, due to known physical restrictions, especially the limited size of displays, data registered by this kind of equipment is limited to qualitative data. This chapter presents an agile method for exploiting desktop eyetracker equipment in combination with mobile devices. The point is coming into play the same facilities used in traditional usability testing in order to obtain also quantitative data. An experimental study has been carried out for two purposes: (1) to prove the efficiency and applicability of proposed method, in comparison to existing options, and (2) to analyze quantitative data extracted from the experiment related to (1) gaze and (2) visual cognition in the exploration of the interface. Findings regarding gaze data are presented.

1.1 Introduction

Due to proven evolution in the mobile application sector, a growing demand exists to explore and innovate in this field, in the line of proposing usability evaluation methodologies specifically adapted for mobile interfaces. Undoubtedly, mobile applications developers must pay a little more special attention to usability.

M. Sendín Veloso (✉) • C. Cuadrat Seix
GRIHO HCI Research Laboratory, University of Lleida, Jaume II, Lleida, Spain
e-mail: msendin@diei.udl.cat; ccuadrat@diei.udl.cat

J.J. Rodríguez Soler
Gneis, Pico S Pedro, Madrid, Spain
e-mail: jjrguezs@bankinter.es

V.M.R. Penichet et al. (eds.), *New Trends in Interaction, Virtual Reality and Modeling,*
Human-Computer Interaction Series, DOI 10.1007/978-1-4471-5445-7_1,
© Springer-Verlag London 2013

Usability methods and principles employed in the evaluation of mobile interfaces are mainly based on techniques and tests traditionally managed in desktop static environments. Furthermore, most of these practices are carried out in controlled environments, thus compromising the mobility factor inherent to this kind of contexts. During the last decade, research in mobile usability has been a new evolving area with few established methodologies and realistic practices that ensure improving usability. Moreover, because of the limited life cycle of this type of development, the rapid change in mobile technology, and an extensively competitive market, these techniques and methodologies are supposed to follow an approach more agile than for traditional interfaces.

This chapter revises the related work in the field of mobile usability evaluation, focusing on the application of eyetracking techniques to mobile usability testing. The challenge of applying eyetracking techniques to mobile interfaces is that these devices screens are too small. To be more precise, at a distance of 50 cm (i.e., the typical distance from the eyes at which a mobile phone is held while using it), only one fixation is necessary for the brain to get an accurate and clear image of approximately a quarter of the display. Hence, using an eyetracker to analyze detailed reading or scanning patterns on a mobile device is difficult, no matter how accurately the eyetracker is able to determine the center of the fixation [11].

This chapter proposes a method that exploits all the potential from the desktop eyetracker by projecting screencasts from mobile interfaces on the eyetracker monitor. The goal is enabling a method for agile and comprehensive mobile usability testing. An experimental study has been carried out in order to prove the adequacy of the proposed method in mobile usability testing. Two different criteria are being considered in the study. Apart from gaze data, collected by the eyetracker, it is intended to validate if there exist significant differences between data regarding the visual task performance obtained from handling the interface on the physical device in relation to the different projection sizes employed in the experiment, as explained henceforth.

The whole purpose is twofold: (1) proposing an evaluation setup for combining the desktop eyetracker with the real usage of mobile devices and (2) facilitating a set of recommendations in the way to use the proposed setup. The central focus is exploiting the quality of gaze data obtained in desktop eyetrackers without compromising the operative veracity in terms of visual cognition performance when using a real device. Our goal is that the conjunction of both issues leads to a valid method for the in-depth study of usability in mobile interfaces.

The next section presents a revision of the related work in mobile usability testing applying eyetracking techniques. Then, the method proposed is presented. In Sect. 1.4, the experimental design conducted is presented, as well as the findings obtained. Finally, some conclusions and future work conclude the chapter.

1.2   State of the Art on Mobile Usability Testing with Eyetracking

There are several reasons that make mobile usability evaluation, and especially the collection of quantitative data challenging, as it is explained in a J. Nielsen's Alertbox.[1] Mobile usability techniques face three main hurdles:

(1) the small screen sizes of mobile devices – this handicap is especially prominent in collecting accurate user's gaze and eye movement data by means of existing eyetracking techniques, and this is because the eye barely moves when a person's gaze shifts between items close together on a small screen [3];
(2) the lack of specific software tools; and
(3) the additional difficulties derived from a mobile context.

In the first place, especially remarkable is the fact that the limited screen size restricts the process of collecting qualitative and quantitative data during usability tests conducted with eyetracking techniques. This is because the eye barely moves when a person's gaze shifts between items close together on a small screen [3], what makes user's gaze and eye movement data collected be little precise.

In the second place, some specific software, such as *Morae* software, cannot take full advantage of its potential when using the mobile device configuration.[2] This software is unable to record the management of the physical device, in comparison to desktop applications, where recording mouse clicks and keyboard usage is allowed.

Finally, the inherent characteristic of mobility associated to mobile devices introduces an extra issue. Considering and incorporating variables regarding the context in the testing process introduces undoubtedly additional challenging points, moving traditional evaluation environments away from a natural situation [7].

Regarding this last point, there has been enormous controversy as to whether results are optimum and relevant when obtained, taking into account mobility and contextual factors in mobile usability tests. This issue has conducted various studies, such as [1, 5–7, 9], contrasting both alternatives, that is, laboratory versus field tests. The conclusions of this research suggest that in most cases the most relevant feedback data is obtained in laboratory studies. Field tests are subject to distractions and interruptions, leading to a drastic reduction of the effective time for evaluation in these kinds of tests. Furthermore, field tests are only able to obtain qualitative data. Moreover, they are likely to detect mainly the most relevant usability problems [5, 6], as well as those mainly related to the device being used, which cannot be found using conventional laboratory tests [1]. In conclusion, such as is recommended in [9], field tests must be carried out in the final stages of development and always after having made at least one laboratory test.

---

[1] http://www.nngroup.com/articles/mobile-usability-first-findings/
[2] http://www.techsmith.com/morae-plugins.html

Fig. 1.1 Eyetracking glasses from SMI (Courtesy of SensoMotoric Instruments GmbH (http://www.eyetracking-glasses.com/))

1.2.1 Eyetracking Techniques Applied with Smartphones

Despite handicaps regarding eyetracking research on mobile usability testing, efforts in this area are growing accordingly[3] [11]. It is this way that there is different eyetracking equipment being commercialized or investigated to be applied in mobile usability evaluation. The following subsections present a revision of different eyetracking equipment employed for mobile devices.

1.2.1.1 Head-Mounted Eyetrackers and Gaze-Based Interactions

Eyetracking glasses are some kind of eyetracking technology – a camera and infrared lights – integrated into the glasses. This equipment can also be provided with recording assistant and infrared markers. Figure 1.1 shows an example.

These glasses are an unobtrusive and lightweight mobile artifact (head-mounted eyetracker) for capturing natural real-world behavior in both qualitative and quantitative research. Automated data mapping and aggregated eyetracking data from several test subjects, along with system-guided procedures, promote process efficiency. These glasses get the information and transmit it via Wi-Fi or bluetooth to the computer connected to the glasses.

Although this method simulates a more natural context of use, information gets lost due to the user who is not usually focused only on looking at the mobile device, as stated in [1]. Furthermore, it does not offer the possibility of mobility in exterior

---

[3]http://www.lt-eval.org/Docs/Thesis-Norlien.pdf

environments, since the data collection device must remain close to the computer. Some eyetracker glasses only record the movement of the real eyes. Most advanced models also record the user's main gaze points, keeping track from eye movement. Anyway, eyetracking glasses do not gather enough data to develop saccade paths or other mapping visualizations, mainly due to the limitations that a reduced display poses on the visual behavior recording.

The external camera inserted in the eyetracker glasses monitors the user interaction with the physical device. However, the user is likely to cover part of the screen with his fingers or hands. These limitations lead to that the results obtained are mainly qualitative.

There are other works in the development of different open-source software and hardware head-mounting eyetracking tools, with which it is possible to log other kind of information data, such as pressing buttons and recording the finger movement on the device screen. Some of the most relevant are the *EyeExpress Tracker* software[4] and the *OpenEyes* project.[5] These projects are still in development and have not presented significant results.

There are other recent developments in mobile eyetracking equipment, in this case oriented at mobile control with the users' eyes. An example is *EyePhone*[6] [8]. It uses the mobile device camera in order to keep track of users via the mobile at hand. This technology is still rudimentary due to their limited object recognition algorithms, which track the position of an eye relative to the screen, rather than where a person is looking at. Apart from limitations in the methodology applied, this technology faces other different main problems derived from mobility and other contextual factors, such as the daylight. Finally, it is worth mentioning that not all the cell phones have a frontal camera, so this method has a strong limitation. Anyway, this method can only be applied to very concrete functionalities, such as selecting an application or an item by blinking, and other similar gaze-based interactions. There are other projects similar to *EyePhone*, such as AOA marker systems [2]. However, none of these projects employs the eyetracking technology for usability purposes.

1.2.1.2 Stand-Alone Eyetracker and Trolleys

Some corporations have developed eyetrackers that can be attached to a mobile trolley. This kind of equipment offers the possibility of doing eyetracking testing introducing some movement, providing more flexibility compared to desktop eyetrackers. Figure 1.2 shows an example of this kind of equipment.

There are two different evaluation setups for this eyetracker equipment: (1) the trolley setup; and (2) the stand-alone setup. The first one offers some mobility,

---

[4]http://xpresstracker.sourceforge.net/

[5]http://thirtysixthspan.com/openEyes/videos.html

[6]http://download.cnet.com/Eye-Phone-Security-Retinal-Scanner/3010-31711_4-75175683.html

Fig. 1.2 Tobii's stand-alone eyetracker (Courtesy of Tobii Technology AB (http://www.tobii.com/en/eye-tracking-research/global/products/hardware/tobii-x60x120-eye-tracker/))

as the trolley can be pushed by users. Despite that, this setup is recommended in controlled environments [11]. An external camera records the user interacting with the physical device.

The stand-alone eyetracker setup uses this eyetracker equipment without the trolley. The eyetracker is positioned upside down in front of the participant so it is able to see straight into the participant's eyes. The device is placed on a table between the eyetracker and the user, who remains completely static sitting in the table. A scene camera is placed on the roof. While it provides the most natural interaction with the device, for the ability of seeing and touching it, this setup is not as flexible as the former. It has important restrictions in the positioning of each one of the test elements. In addition, the user must always keep his view centered on the mobile device, a position that is no longer comfortable and flexible for the user. Figure 1.3 depicts this setup.

With this eyetracker equipment, technologically more potent than the eyetracker glasses, both qualitative and quantitative data can be obtained [11]. However, as in the case of eyetracker glasses, the limitations of reduced screens complicate the visualization of the interaction, without forgetting the handicaps of gaze data recording. Moreover, both setups are complicated to arrange because of its build complexity [11].

1.2.1.3 Desktop Monitor-Based Eyetrackers

The desktop monitor-based eyetracker consists in a desktop screen that includes all the eyetracking equipment, incorporated video camera, and infrared light sensors.

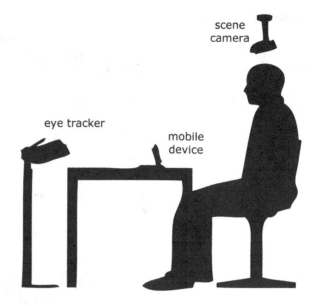

Fig. 1.3 The stand-alone eyetracker setup shown in [11] (Courtesy of Tobii Technology AB)

This equipment allows a high degree of head movement, and the software records all the mouse inputs and keyboard interaction. The user interaction is completely recorded, so there is no need for an external camera.

Unlike the equipment presented above, it has a high degree of accuracy and quality of recording when tracking the eye. Among other things, the user has a larger screen size where eyes require extensive movements. Reliability in research results regarding gaze data is ensured. Moreover, being a computer screen, it is easier for the user to focus on the screen. Figure 1.4 shows a model.

So far, two different setups and methodologies for desktop eyetracker have been developed for mobile devices: (1) the emulator setup; and (2) the configuration known as the below table setup. Both of them are detailed henceforth.

1.2.1.4   Emulator Setup

The emulator setup involves installing an emulator in the eyetracker computer for the target smartphone, so that the user interacts with it as if it was a common computer application. Figure 1.6 shows a capture from an emulator.

This is the simplest way of carrying out eyetracking tests for mobile interfaces. Accurate and significant qualitative and quantitative eyetracking data can be collected, as it brings into play all the eyetracking potential, including the possibility of logging clicks [11]. However, there are various problems.

First of all, the user does not interact with the mobile device itself, but with an emulator, which makes the interaction unnatural. So this kind of testing cannot provide feedback on how users would interact with the actual three-dimensional

Fig. 1.4 Tobii's desktop monitor-based eyetracker (Courtesy of Tobii Technology AB (http://www. tobii.com/en/eye-tracking-research/global/products/ hardware/tobii-t60t120-eye-tracker/))

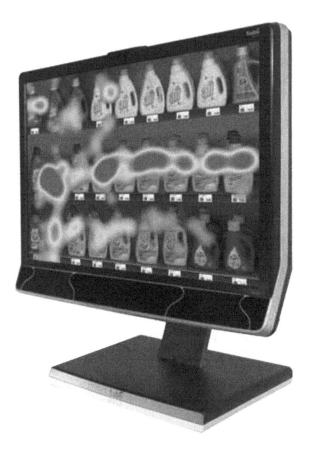

device. Instead of using the interaction style from the device, the user interacts with the keyboard and mouse. It is worth mentioning, however, that this setup can be combined with a touch screen overlay to provide a more natural interaction, as explained in [11]. Secondly, many emulators are slower than the device itself, since they consume machine resources, while the computer machine is also supporting the eyetracker software. This can lead to latency issues. Thirdly, the visualization of emulators has certain limitations regarding the screen display. The user is viewing a window with approximately the same size as the mobile screen, but it is farther away than the device itself if the user was using it. Finally, it is worth mentioning the lack of realism in the use of emulators. An emulator is just pretending, not actually running, the hardware and software abilities and constraints unique to a given device.

Fig. 1.5 The below table
setup showed in [11]
(Courtesy of Tobii
Technology AB)

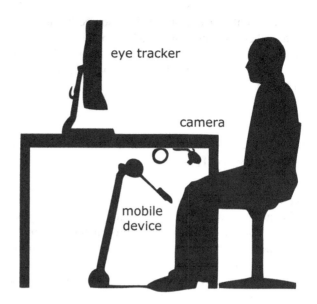

1.2.1.5   The Below Table Setup

This setup consists in installing a foot under the table on which the mobile device lies, along with a camera that monitors onto the eyetracker screen all the actions being undertaken by the user with the device. Figure 1.5 depicts this setup.

As in the previous case, using this setup both significant qualitative and quantitative data can be obtained, as it brings into play all the eyetracking potential [11]. However, there are also some complications regarding the user interaction.

The first inconvenience is that although the user interacts with the mobile device itself, what makes this setup very natural in terms of physical interaction, he stays in an uncomfortable and unnatural position. The user must keep his hands under the table all the time. It must also be taken into consideration the discomfort caused by visualizing all the changes performed on the device's screen by means of a camera capture on the eyetracker monitor. The user's natural tendency is to look directly at the device. This fact can lead to the user looking away from the eyetracker monitor, looking for the device in his hands under the table, conducting to an unnatural visual interaction with the device [11]. It is well known that having to work with a capture of the device from a video camera consequently introduces major limitations regarding size, resolution and image quality.

Moreover, such as in the case of the stand-alone setup, it is quite complex to carry out. On the one hand, it is necessary to modify the setup according to every user's needs and configure it to prevent light sources from causing reflections on the screen. On the other hand, users need to have previous training, as stated in [11], regarding the coordination of their fingers in relation to the feedback from the camera. For these reasons, users must first be properly informed of the inconveniences before starting the test.

1.3 Proposed Method for Quantitative Mobile Usability Testing

The last section has presented existing problems in the application of eyetracking techniques in mobile usability testing. The factors exposed highlight a remarkable need for further technological improvement in eyetracking techniques and equipment specific for mobile devices. The most worrying point is ensuring reliability in quantitative data regarding users' visual behavior. The desktop monitor-based eyetrackers are the most reliable in order to acquire both quantitative and qualitative data. Nevertheless, setups presented have some difficult issues. This section presents an agile and comprehensive method for quantitative mobile usability testing applying traditional desktop eyetracking techniques.

The key point to obtain fully benefits from a desktop eyetracker is somehow facilitating a complete deployment of the mobile interface on the monitor, as realistically as possible. We are referring to displaying a live video projection of the mobile interface, and at the same time controlling it directly from the desktop, by using its input peripherals. This way is ensured that the participant remains looking at the eyetracker monitor during the ongoing testing, so that the application of the eyetracking techniques can be exploited. Screencasting must be obtained without incurring in time latency in the performance of the mobile interface.

The study realized has been focused on the Android OS. For this OS, the screencasting can be obtained using diverse open-source applications. Some of them were discarded due to a slow refresh rate, which poses latency problems. Finally, the alternative selected has been the MyMobiler software utility for diverse reasons. MyMobiler allows connecting and controlling the device both via the USB cable and via Wi-Fi. As it has been previously stated, enlarging the display compared to the actual size of mobile devices screens helps getting accurate gaze data [11]. Keeping this in mind, one of the main requirements for selecting the screencast utility to be applied was the possibility of scaling the projection of the mobile interface. MyMobiler allows scaling it among diverse sizes, unlike some of the utilities tested. However, it has to be taken into account that it requires having the device rooted, which implies making root permissions available on the device.

1.4 Experimental Study

In this section, the most relevant points regarding the experimental study conducted to validate the presented method are described. Findings from the analysis carried out up to now are shown to conclude it.

As stated in our previous work [4], the starting point comes with two assumptions: (1) the quality of gaze data can be affected by variations in the size of projection and (2) these variations can also affect users' performance in visual skill tasks, trying to go further in verifying the proposed method, in the line of visual cognition studies. Our purpose is searching the impact that variations in the projected image have in the users' visual performance.

During the experiment, data regarding these two points was collected. For assumption (1), two eyetracking metrics have been involved in our analysis: the fixation duration mean[7] and the number of fixations.[8] In relation to assumption (2), some values have been registered regarding the completion time in the execution of a certain visual task, as well as other variables related to participants' visual skill. The present chapter is focused on validating the proposed method regarding the first assumption.

1.4.1 Participants

To recruit participants in the experiment, no specific user profile was selected. The intention was to recruit a varied sample as much as possible in terms of age, gender, visual condition, and their experience with smartphone usage. Before the experiment, a demographic questionnaire was filled in by the participants. Forty-two participants took part in the experiment. They were between 17 and 54 years old (31 in average). There were 28 men and 14 women. More details about the other considered features from participants (visual condition and their experience with smartphone usage) can be looked up in [4].

1.4.2 Experimental Design

In order to overcome the fact that the eyetracker equipment used in this experiment was not provided with the touch screen overlay complement, another interactive support was introduced explicitly in the experiment: a desktop touch screen. The aim

---

[7]A cumulative duration of consecutive fixations within an area of interest. Typically includes several fixations and may include a relatively small amount of time for the short saccades between them [10].

[8]The amount of visual fixations registered.

Table 1.1 Experimental design

	Factor B		
Factor B	a1. Eyetracker	a2. Touchscreen	a3. Mobile phone
b1. Reference size			Y_{31}
b2. Size 1	Y_{12}	Y_{21}	
b3. Size 2	Y_{13}	Y_{23}	
b4. Size 3	Y_{14}	Y_{24}	

was homogenizing the interaction style between the physical device and the mobile interface projection, providing a faithful interaction experience. It is also remarkable that the desktop touch screen showed a more agile response time than the eyetracker equipment. This fact also helped in equating times between the desktop support and the physical mobile device.

Thereby, the experiment consisted of three different stages with a different interactive support in each: (1) the desktop eyetracker (a Tobii T60[9]), (2) the desktop touch screen (a Sony VAIO SJ[10]), and (3) the mobile device (an HTC Desire[11]). In the case of the desktop equipment – (1) and (2) – participants performed the task with three projection sizes, which correspond to the following increments on the real device screen: 32.6, 95.2, and 161.5 mm, respectively, for sizes ×1, ×2, and ×3 (increased on average by 96.4 mm).

Completion time data was extracted from the desktop touch screen in order to be contrasted with those from the mobile device during the performance of visual skills. The goal is to determine which projection size in the touch screen is closer to the physical device in terms of visual skill performance, in response to the second assumption. Consequently, the eyetracker was only focused on registering the visual behavior from participants. Gaze data and visual performance tasks are going to be analyzed by a separate study and then confronted by each other in order to establish a relationship between variables handled in two assumptions.

According to the variables presented above, a nested two-factor experimental design with repeated measures or within subject was chosen. Factor A refers to the type of interactive support with which participants executed the experimental task. Factor B refers to different projection sizes of the interface, as shown in Table 1.1.

To control the external effects, such as learning effect, attributable to within-subject designs, we established several experimental control mechanisms: (1) random variations in the order of use of each one of the interactive supports (Factor A) and (2) random variations in sizes of projection (Factor B).

Finally, participants were asked to fill in a questionnaire in order to find out with which projection size they felt more comfortable.

---

[9]http://www.tobii.com/Global/Analysis/Downloads/User_Manuals_and_Guides/Tobii_T60_T120_EyeTracker_UserManual.pdf

[10]http://www.sony.es/product/vd-j-series

[11]http://www.htc-desire.es/htc-desire/

1.4.3 Procedure

One of the goals set during the study was to verify the suitability of this method through external validity criteria. These criteria seek establishing a correlation between eyetracking measures and visual performance tasks.

Keeping these objectives in mind, an application for Android OS based on location strategies and visual exploration consisting in locating a visual target stimulus from an array of distracting stimuli was designed. To be more precise, the goal is finding a unique letter hidden in a six-by-six matrix of numbers over a given number of times – essays – in each execution of the task. Distracting stimuli are the random arrays of numbers, and the target stimuli are the unique letter, whose position in the matrix is also random. Each cell of the matrix is framed by selectable buttons. Thus, pressing a button causes stepping to the next essay and registering the corresponding success or error.

More details about this application, which was the experimental task assigned to the participants, can be looked up in [4]. It was designed in order to realize and log different essays. At the end of the test, a complete log of the times taken in each essay, in conjunction with a summary of successes and errors, is displayed and also sent via e-mail in *csv* (comma-separated values) format.

1.4.4 Data Analysis

In this section findings regarding the first assumption are presented.

As it can be observed in Fig. 1.6, which illustrate the saccade paths obtained for the three projection sizes from a same participant, two first observations can be made, which are in concordance with numerical data: (a) *the smaller the projection is, the longer the fixation duration mean* (greater circles for fixations). According to this, (b) *the smaller projection has less number of fixations than the other two ones.* These results are also illustrated quantitatively by means of two graphics in [4], which show the results of the means for the two eyetracking metrics applied to each group. These observations are consistent with literature [11]: in the smallest projection participants required less eye movement to be able to find the letter.

In order to support both observations, an analysis of variance (ANOVA) was made in which the two statements annunciated above – (a) and (b) – which are related to the two eyetracking metrics involved in the first assumption, were the two hypotheses for the study (H_1 and H_2 respectively). As it can be looked up in [4], the ANOVA test determined that there are statistically significant differences between group means for both variables involved. Therefore, variations in the projection sizes influence both on the fixation duration mean and on the number of fixations.

A multiple comparisons post hoc test for both metrics in order to determine which means cause the differences between groups has been carried out. The test applied was Scheffé statistic through the SPSS software.

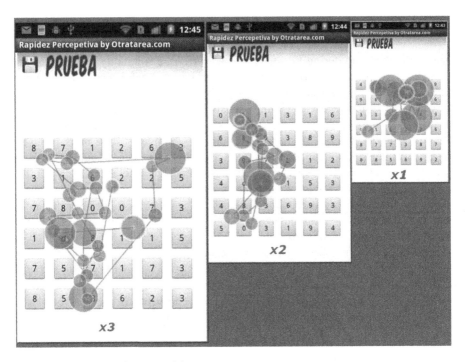

Fig. 1.6 Saccade paths from a participant

As it is shown in Table 1.2, significant differences (P < = 0.05) were found for both metrics, the fixation duration and the number of fixations when projecting different sizes of images. However, we have found that the trends are different for each variable.

In the case of the fixation duration metric, we found significant differences when comparing the ×1 size with the ×2 and ×3 sizes (P = 0.001 and P = 0.00, respectively). These results can be interpreted thus: "as the size of the projections increases, the duration of fixations decreases." However, we did not find statistically significant differences (P = 0.378) when comparing sizes ×2 and ×3. For this reason, we cannot conclude that the trend was found linear. In other words, the changes in the projection sizes are influencing differently in the fixation duration.

In the case of the number of fixations, we also found significant differences comparing the size ×1 with the sizes ×2 and ×3 (P = 0.003 and P = 0.014, respectively). However, these differences are of the opposite sign. In other words, "with a smaller projection size, the user does a fewer number of fixations". Similarly to the previous case, no significant differences were found between the sizes ×2 and ×3 in order to ensure the linearity of this trend in all comparisons. Further, unlike what was observed for the fixation duration, for the number of fixations variable, this trend is broken, turning to the same sign as for the first variable between the ×2 and ×3 sizes. Figure 1.7 shows these tendencies for both variables: (a) the fixation duration and (b) the number of fixations.

Table 1.2 Analysis of the influence of varying sizes on eyetracking variable

Multiple comparisons

Scheffe

Dependent variable	(I) Image projection size	(J) Image projection size	Mean difference (I-J)	Std error	Sig	95 % confidence interval Lower bound	Upper bound
Duration of fixation	x1	x2	0.08905[a]	0.02226	0.001	0.0339	0.1442
		x3	0.12024[a]	0.02226	0.000	0.0651	0.1754
	x2	x1	−0.08905[a]	0.02226	0.001	−0.1442	−0.0339
		x3	0.03119	0.02226	0.378	−0.0240	0.0863
	x3	x1	−0.12024[a]	0.02226	0.000	−0.1754	−0.0651
		x2	−0.03119	0.02226	0.378	−0.0863	0.0240
Number of Fixation	x1	x2	−47.76190[a]	13.70849	0.003	−81.7296	−13.7942
		x3	−40.71429[a]	13.70849	0.014	−74.6820	−6.7466
	x2	x1	47.76190[a]	13.70849	0.003	13.7942	81.7296
		x3	7.04762	13.70849	0.876	−26.9201	41.0513
	x3	x1	40.71429[a]	13.70849	0.014	6.7466	74.6820
		x2	−7.04762	13.70849	0.876	−41.0153	26.9201

[a]The mean difference is significant at the 0.5 level

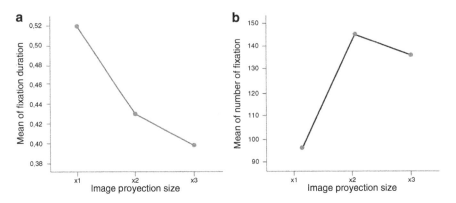

Fig. 1.7 Trends in the evolution of the two variables regarding the different projection sizes

1.5 Conclusions and Future Work

The great impact in the use of mobile devices in daily life reveals the need for defining effective mobile usability testing. In particular, eyetracking techniques have some crucial problems regarding physical device limitations. An alternative method (an evaluation setup and a set of recommendations) has been presented based on desktop eyetracker. The first part of data analysis resulting from the experiment conducted to validate it has been concluded and presented in this chapter.

Results regarding the first assumption conclude that the quality of gaze data is affected by variations in the size of projection, as enunciated in the literature [11]. To be more precise, enlarging the projection size, the visual behavior from participants can be studied in a greater level of detail because more precise data information in the obtaining of visual details is obtained. In order to obtain concluding results in the line of determining the optimal size (×2, ×3, or some other between them) in terms of effectiveness, a further analysis is required. For that, a statistic analysis regarding the second assumption is being run, as the second part of this study. The goal is studying how variations in the projection sizes can affect users' performance in visual skill tasks. Finally, a study of correlation between eyetracking measures with those obtained from visual skill data is going to be done. Additionally, another experiment is being planned to be held using the ×2 and ×3 projection sizes, applying some variations in the experimental design in the line of controlling some extra external variables. It is worthy to do a further analysis in the line of finding out why trends change when the projection size changes from ×2 to ×3 in the number of fixations variable, as well as why different trends are occurring in different variables. We are planning to use a different mobile application in the next experiment.

Comparing the proposed method with the practices analyzed in Sect. 1.2, it is worthy to say that there is a compromise between efficiency and naturality (real experience with the physical device) in the use of the mobile device. The proposed method prioritizes efficiency. Moreover, the impact from lack of naturality is partially compensated by applying the screencasting utility, gaining thus in visual realism, as well as using a touch overly complement. There are also overall advantages for proposed method, some of them derived from using the desktop equipment, which can be looked up in [4]. Finally, regarding the agility in the application of the method, it is highly integratable in UCD (user-centered design) processes, not only because it offers a "light" method but also because it can be applied since the early stages in development. To conclude, even though the method needs further analysis, this first analysis provides a good starting point towards its validation as a comprehensive and agile method for quantitative mobile usability testing, which not only seems to be a valid way to overcome the lack of quality in gaze data but also presents numerous benefits.

As further work, new explorations in mobile usability testing are planned to be covered. On the one hand, the proposed method opens the door to new types of devices, such as tablets. On the other hand, it is planned to apply this method in the implementation of field tests in real scenarios.

References

1. Been-Lirn Duh, H., Tan, C. B., & Hsueh-hua, V. (2006). Usability evaluation for mobile device: A comparison of laboratory and field tests. In *Proceedings of MobileHCI'06* (pp. 181–186). Espoo: Finland. doi: 10.1145/1152215.1152254.
2. Brone, G., Oben, B., & Goedeme, T. (2011). Towards a more effective method for analyzing mobile eye-tracking data: integrating gaze data with object recognition algorithms. In *Proceeding of PETMEI'11* (pp. 1–4). Beijing. doi: 10.1145/2029956.2029971.
3. Cheng, S. (2011). The research framework of eyetracking based mobile device usability evaluation. In *Proceeding of PETMEI'11* (pp. 21–26). Beijing: ACM. doi: 10.1145/2029956.2029964.
4. Cuadrat, C., Sendín, M., & Rodríguez, J. J. (2012). Towards the validation of a method for quantitative mobile usability testing based on desktop eyetracking. In *Actas del XIII Congreso Internacional de Interacción Persona-Ordenador*. New York: ACM. ISBN: 978-1-4503-1314-8. doi: 10.1145/2379636.2379684.
5. Elzakker, C., Delikostidis, I., & Oosterom, P. (2011). Field-based usability evaluation methodology for mobile geo-applications. *The Cartographic Journal, 45*(2), 139–149. doi:10.1179/174327708x305139.
6. Kaikkonen, A., Kallio, T., Kekäläinen, A., Kankainen, A., & Cankar, M. (2005). Usability testing of mobile applications: A comparison between laboratory and field testing. *Journal of Usability Studies, 1*(1), 4–16. doi:10.1234/12345678.
7. Kjeldskov, J., Graham, C., Pedell, S., Vetere, F., Howard, S., Balbo, R., & Davies, J. (2005). Evaluating the usability of a mobile guide: The influence of location, participants and resources. *Journal of the Behavior and Information Technology, 24*, 51–65. doi:10.1080/01449290512331319030.
8. Miluzzo, E., Wang, T., & Campbell, A. T. (2010). EyePhone: Activating mobile phones with your eyes. In *MobiHeld 2010* (pp. 15–20). New Delhi: ACM. doi: 10.1145/1851322.1851328.
9. Nielsen, C. M., Overgaard, M., Pedersen, M. B., Stage, J., & Stenild, S. (2006). It's worth the hassle! The added value of evaluating the usability of mobile systems in the field. In *NordiCHI'06* (pp. 272–280). Oslo: ACM. doi: 10.1145/1182475.1182504.
10. Poole, A., & Ball, L. J. (2007). Eye tracking in human-computer interaction and usability research: Current status and future prospects. In C. Ghaoui (Ed.), *Encyclopedia of human computer interaction*. Pennsylvania: Idea Group.
11. Tobii Technology.WhitePaper: Using Eye Tracking to Test Mobile Devices (2012) What to consider and how to set it up. http://www.tobii.com/Global/Analysis/Training/WhitePapers/Tobii_Using_EyeTracking_to_Test_Mobile_Devices_WhitePaper.pdf. Accessed Jan 2012.

Chapter 2
An Approach to Explore Large-Scale Collections Based on Classification Schemes

María Auxilio Medina Nieto, Jorge de la Calleja Mora, Antonio Benitez Ruiz, and J. Alfredo Sánchez

Abstract This chapter describes an approach to explore large-scale collections based on classification systems. We have called this approach as SV, an acronym for scheme visualization. SV is implemented as a set of SVG charts. A two-dimensional interface maps the main and secondary categories in the x- and y-axes, respectively. The use of color, size, place, and shape in the interface has a predefined intention. The chapter reports preliminary results of our prototype version to explore CORTUPP, a collection of documents classified with the 1998 ACM Computing Classification System.

2.1 Introduction

In digital libraries, *classification schemes* are used to access, index, and query collections; they organize documents in hierarchies of subjects or categories. The more specific a subject is, the deeper level assigned to it. The Dewey Decimal Classification (DDC), the Library of Congress Classification (LCC), and the Universal Decimal Classification (UDC) are common classification schemes. Often, subjects have an identifier formed by numbers, letters, or a blend of both.

Interoperability mechanisms such as the Open Archives Initiative Protocol for Metadata Harvesting (OAI-PMH protocol) use at a minimum the elements of

M.A. Medina Nieto (✉) • J. de la Calleja Mora • A. Benitez Ruiz
Laboratorio de Percepción por Computadora, Universidad Politécnica de Puebla, Tercer Carril del Ejido Serrano S/N San Mateo Cuanalá, Juan C. Bonilla, Puebla, Mexico
e-mail: mauxmedina@gmail.com; jorgedelacalleja@gmail.com; antonio.benitez@uppuebla.edu.mx

J.A. Sánchez
Human-Computer Interaction Laboratory, Universidad de las Américas – Puebla, Ex-hacienda Santa Catarina Mártir S/N, San Andrés Cholula, Puebla, Mexico
e-mail: j.alfredo.sanchez@gmail.com

V.M.R. Penichet et al. (eds.), *New Trends in Interaction, Virtual Reality and Modeling*, Human-Computer Interaction Series, DOI 10.1007/978-1-4471-5445-7_2, © Springer-Verlag London 2013

unqualified Dublin Core (DC) metadata format to disseminate collections. Besides the use of data and metadata by search engines, visualization schemes represent another accessibility alternative for collections. These schemes try to capture intellectual structures perceived in a particular domain of knowledge.

This chapter describes SV, an approach to explore large-scale collections. A two-dimensional interface based on SVG[1] charts allows users to have a high-level overview of categories in a classification scheme and the distribution of documents in a collection. We assumed that documents are classified.

The chapter is organized as follows: the next section presents related work. Our visualization approach is described in Sect. 2.3. We exchange views on preliminary results at Sect. 2.4. Finally, we include conclusions and suggest future directions of our work in Sect. 2.5.

2.2   Related Work

In digital libraries, users, librarians, and documentalists have tools as search engines to locate information. We believe that the way they obtain information is decisive to their exploration. This section describes some significant related works with the visualization of collections in two or three dimensions. In OntoStarFish interface, users can organize documents by keywords, subjects, or collaborators. Subjects are predefined categories but subcategories are automatically extracted by using a clustering algorithm. The clustering algorithm is presented in [2]; an adaptation of it to OAI[2] records can be found in [3]. In the two-dimensional interface of OntoStarFish, the x-axis shows subject categories, while the y-axis displays buttons to select a country, which is a value for a specific metadata. In this work, other metadata such as title, author, or publisher are also used to navigate the collections.

Figure 2.1 shows an excerpt of OntoStarFish interface when the user chooses Mexico, the subject "medicine," and two fish eyes. The number of multiple fish-eye views is introduced by the user in a select box. A square is used for each subject that contains documents. The set of documents are represented as filled circles in the interface. The size of each dot is related with the number of selected documents.

The following related works make use of a widely known classification scheme for computer science documents referred as the 1998 ACM Computing Classification System (abbreviated CCS) [4]. CCS has 11 main categories and 72 subcategories organized in a four-level taxonomy. The categories use identifiers that are formed as follows: at the first level, identifiers use a capital letter from A to K;

---

[1]SVG is the abbreviation for Scalable Vector Graphics, which is an XML-based vector image format for two-dimensional graphics that has support for interactivity and animation.

[2]The Open Archives Initiative is an organization that promotes interoperability standards to disseminate content in digital libraries.

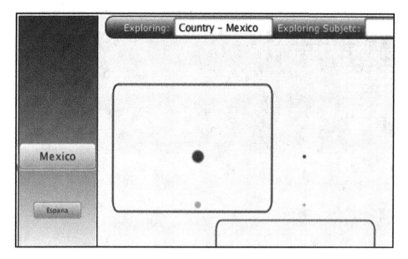

Fig. 2.1 An excerpt of OntoStarFish visualization

at the second one the identifier is formed by a letter, a period, and a number or the *m* letter. An additional number is used at the third level. Categories at the fourth level do not use identifiers; instead, they represent an ordered list of general terms and proper nouns.

Authors of [5] describe a visual survey tool developed in JavaScripts that allow users to select subjects to construct a tree that displays the first three levels of CCS. Main categories are displayed at the top of the interface. Once users choose a category, a rectangle at the center of the interface shows the respective tree. Rectangles with the codes of categories are linked with lines to represent the complete hierarchy. A tooltip effect is added to display the cluster label on the rectangles of categories at the third level. The interface allows users to access documents from the trees and shows the percentage of documents for category. Users need to choose category names before accessing the documents. From our point of view, that order of tasks represents a disadvantage due to documents that need to be classified using at least a subcategory of the third level before they can be accessed in the interface; therefore, documents only classified with a category or subcategory would not be visible.

Technical Report Visualizer System (TRV) uses open standards to show classification metadata in the interface. This uses the OAI Protocol for Metadata Harvesting (OAI-PMH) to gather the metadata of arXiv e-Print articles at Cornell University [6]. Subjects are displayed in a Java hyperbolic tree with hyperlinks to full text.

Hyperbolic views are recommended to show large non-balance hierarchies. User navigation activity is combined to access the abstracts or full-text contents of articles classified with CCS categories. The nodes with more documents have a higher intensity color and a wider border. The number of citations of a node is indicated in square brackets as a suffix to the node label. TVR uses Xerces, Xalan, DOM,

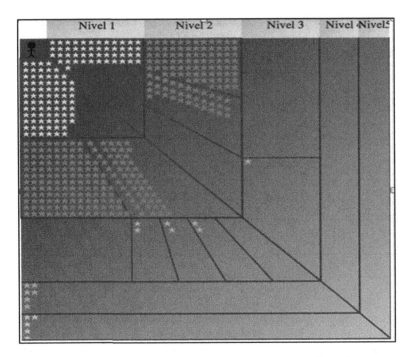

Fig. 2.2 A visualization interface for CORTUPP based on an ontology of records

SAX, and other XML-based technologies to support visualization and browsing. The visualization technique used in TVR takes into account similarity measures between documents based on cites.

We have explored the visualization of collections in [7, 8]. Documents are automatically organized in a structure referred to as an *ontology of records*. This structure is the result of applying an adaptation of FIHC algorithm to a set of documents [2]. FIHC requires three input parameters to construct a tree of disjoint clusters in an off-line mode. Clusters at the first level have a label with one term; clusters at the second level have a label with two terms, the term of their ancestor category and a new term; and so on.

Figure 2.2 shows a section of a web page that visualizes an ontology of records for a collection of documents of the Universidad Politécnica de Puebla called CORTUPP. A blue gradient background that is darker at the first level and lighter at the latest one is used as a visual effect to represent the hierarchical relationships between levels. The interface shows the first five levels. A label with the number of each level is shown in green buttons.

Documents are represented as stars; those are constructed as independent files in such a way that any other symbol can be used to satisfy user preferences. Another visual features of this scheme are the following ones:

- The smallest square at the left top corner has an icon with a person to point to the root of the ontology of records.
- Each level is subdivided to show sibling clusters.
- Stars are displayed in different colors, one for each level. A slight variation of size is also used.

From our point of view, the main disadvantage of the interface in Fig. 2.1 is related with the name of the classes in the ontology of records and their relationships with ontology levels. The classes and subclasses in classification schemes often have a name that does not share a set of terms. Thus, we decided to work with a visualization approach that incorporates the main features of classification. The following section describes the proposed visualization scheme.

2.3   SV Approach

This section describes SV, a visualization approach formed by a two-dimensional interface based on SVG charts to explore large-scale collections of classified documents. SV is an acronym for "scheme visualization"; it also coincides with the first two letters of SVG. We assume that each document of a collection is stored as an OAI-PMH record and that each document is classified according to a predefined classification scheme that uses identifiers. Each record can belong to more than a class in the same branch of the classification scheme; however, a unique representation in the deeper level of the interface is suggested in order to avoid redundancy.

In the proposed approach, we follow the design principles proposed by [9]:

- Offer information feedback
- Reduce working memory load
- Provide alternative interfaces for novice and expert users

2.3.1   Data Sets

The values of *dc:subject* elements of records are associated with a category of a classification scheme. These values can be written in multiple languages such as English and Spanish in order to improve collection accessibility. Table 2.1 shows the elements used in SV. Note that any other collection that represent documents as OAI records can use DC elements in a similar way. The cardinality column refers to the number of occurrences of an element in an OAI-PMH record. An example of an OAI-PMH record is available at http://informatica.uppuebla.edu.mx/oai-uppuebla/ontoairGetRecord.xml

We suggest a unique value for each DC element in such a way that multiple values require multiple instances of the elements. As a way of illustration, if a

Table 2.1 Use of DC elements in SV

DC element	Description	Cardinality
dc:contributor	The full name of a member on an assessment committee	At least one, the maximum is three
dc:coverage	The degree of the dc:author (BEng degree or MSc degree)	Only one
dc:date	The delivery date of the document	Only one
dc:format	The MIME[a] type (application/pdf)	Only one
dc:identifier	The OAI-PMH identifier of the document	Only one
dc:language	The language of the content of the document (Spanish)	At least one
dc:publisher	The full name of the UPPuebla	Only one
dc:source	The link to access full-text document	At least one
dc:subject	The identifier and the name of a category in a classification scheme	At least one
dc:title	The title of the document	Only one
dc:type	The type of the document	Only one

[a] *MIME* multipurpose Internet mail extensions

document has four authors, four instances of the *dc:contributor* element will be expected. We also take into account that each element only has one value. Besides the metadata of Table 2.1, a link to access the full-text document of each record is commonly used in visualization schemes.

Collections can store different types of documents. For example, CORTUPP has technical reports, articles, and theses. The value of a *dc:type* element can be used to store those types.

2.3.2 Visualization Strategy

In this work, the visualization strategy is realized with SVG charts, an XML-based technology to create two- and three-dimensional web graphics. In general, vector formats provide quality, scalability, and extensibility that cannot be obtained in raster images. Other advantages of this official W3C standard are search ability, dynamism, and update ability.

SVG has been used to visualize metadata, ontologies, and other types of conceptual structures for human meanings [10]. SVG format stores structural information about graphical shapes as an integral part of the image. This information can be processed by other technologies to increase accessibility, especially when this information is complemented by metadata.

As a way of illustration, the following code shows an excerpt of the type of information that can be included in a SVG file. These lines produce the background and a star from Fig. 2.2. Note that colors and basic changes can be made even by nonexpert users in order to satisfy some preferences:

```
<linearGradient id="marino_cielo" x1="0%" y1="0%"
                x2="100%" y2="100%">
    <stop offset="0%"
    style="stop-color:darkblue;stop-opacity:0.9.5"/>
    <stop offset="100%" style="stop-color:deepskyblue;
    stop-opacity:0.5"/>
</linearGradient>
<symbol id="estrella">
<polygon points="186,104 233,104 250,60 267,104 314,
104 280,138 304,190 250,158 196,190 220,138"
style="fill:gold;stroke:orange; stroke-width:4"/>
</symbol>
```

SVG supports the separation of structure and information from style and presentation, as suggested in the Web Content Accessibility Guidelines.[3]

2.3.3   Visual Attributes

A web interface and SVG charts are the main components of the proposed visualization scheme. An organization based on top, left, and right frames is used. The top frame displays a title and the objective of the interface. The frame on the left allows users to explore the collection and visualize the relationships between CCS categories before accessing document metadata. The frame on the right shows metadata in a HTML page with some basic style elements. Category names can be visualized in this frame. Figure 2.3 shows the interface for SV tool. In order to put reader's attention on the graphical elements, we only show the second frame. The navigation and its events are handled as follows:

1. A user chooses a row and a column to show the documents at the first category (as the red legend on the left suggest) and a column for the respective subcategory (this is expressed in a green legend that appears on the top of the interface).
2. Once that the user clicks a rectangle, the user can access to documents or to explore the third level. The rectangles are used to represent sets of documents as a metaphor commonly used in the exploration of files of many operative systems. Note that the number of rectangles that appear on the left in a row is the same as the number of subcategories. The column of rectangles on the right is used to represent groups of documents that can be considered as belonging to more than a subcategory, which is often called as hybrid or miscellaneous clusters.

---

[3]Authoring Tool Accessibility Guidelines 1.0., J. Treviranus, C. McCathieNevile, I. Jacobs, and J. Richards, eds., 3 February 2000. Available at: http://www.w3.org/TR/2000/REC-ATAG10-20000203

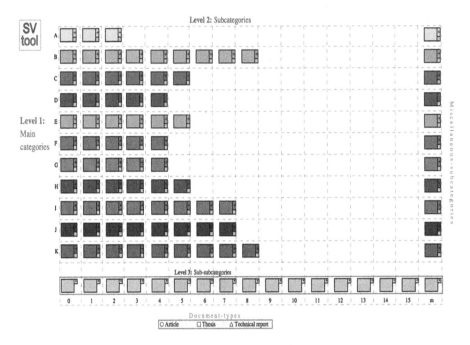

Fig. 2.3 The main interface of SV

The design process takes into account the size, shape, color, and localization of the elements. The two-dimensional display uses categorical axes. The columns are associated with the main categories and the rows with the subcategories. Each category has a label (a CCS code), a level, and zero or more documents. Color coding is used to associate documents with the main categories (which are identified by the letters in black color on the left side). The plus icon at the right corner of each rectangle shows the metadata of the documents and the category description. A hyperlink points to the full-text files.

All the documents that belong to a main category are placed inside the rectangles. If a main category has more than six documents, then a new SVG graphic is displayed in another window of the browser. Thus, at first glance, each square shows a maximum of six records. Square, triangle, and circle icons represent a type of document. In the case of CORTUPP, three types of documents are used: articles, theses, and technical reports, represented with a circle, a square, and a triangle, respectively. The visualization of some documents in SV tool is illustrated in Fig. 2.4, which is a zoom view of the left corner of Fig. 2.3. The first row shows six documents for three subcategories and three documents for the miscellaneous category of the first main category A, which is "general literature."

We use the same background color for the square of the category and square with the plus symbol and a gray background for accessing the following level of subcategories (level 3). The squares that have an m letter instead of a plus symbol

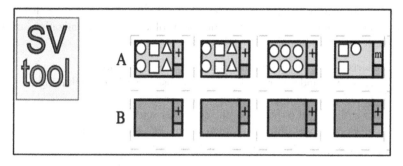

Fig. 2.4 Representation of documents in a main category

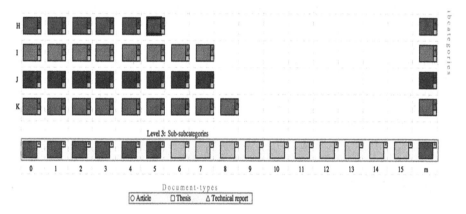

Fig. 2.5 Visualization of documents at the third level

are used for "miscellaneous categories." The rest of documents are displayed by pressing the plus symbol on the right of each square.

A web page has been designed to explore SV. Properties' files support flexibility aspects such as customization of colors, style and size of fonts, and background color. The shapes used to represent the types of documents can be modified without significant changes in the SVG code.

Figure 2.5 shows a screenshot of the interface for a respondent who chose an icon that access to a document associated to a category at the third level. Note that a different set of icons is used to represent the types of documents. User interaction with the interface can be useful to learn the organization of computer science. The gray rectangles at the top are used to display categories at level 3. Observe that these rectangles were allocated at the bottom on Fig. 2.5, but we have moved them in order to attract reader's attention. A subcategory is displayed in the same color as its main category. The black lines show explicitly the relationships on the chosen categories. Only a subcategory at the third level can be chosen at the same time.

The style of a color palette was proposed in order to emphasize the existence of different and disjoint categories. From our point of view, our visualization scheme offers the following advantages:

- SVG charts can be displayed on different devices and platform.
- SVG is a W3C standard; this allows users to use other XML technologies.
- SVG avoids long or complex sentence structures.
- We offer a high-level overview of the computer science domain.
- SV tool is an accessibility alternative for large-scale collections classified with CCS. SV tool provides easy identification of explored and unexplored categories in an organization. It could be useful to plan research restructuring and investment.
- SV tool enables simultaneous visualization of different kind of documents.
- SV provides access to metadata without the lost of contextual navigation.
- SV incorporates metadata in SVG charts for future applications.

Some limitations of the current version are the following: (1) there is no information about the number of elements that a category has (in the current version the number of documents that a category can contain is restricted by the size of the rectangle that represents it in the interface) and (2) the size of the squares is fixed. Given server overhead or the bandwidth restriction, it may be appropriate to generate the SVG charts in advance periodically.

2.3.4 Technical Aspects

Xerces is the Java parser used for metadata extraction of records. SVG charts are constructed online in a Java application; after that, they are incorporated into a web-accessible directory. SVG version 1.1 is used. Some browsers could require an SVG plug-in.

2.4 Preliminary Results

A problem to evaluate different visualization schemes of textual information is the difficulty to compare the efficiency between different solutions. We have applied some techniques on our prototype version for a preliminary evaluation of SV. We have designed tasks related to the interpretation of CCS categories in the proposed interface and the identification of explored and unexplored categories based on the document membership. Pre- and posttest questionnaires were applied to 20 users to obtain feedback. A 1–5 Likert-type scale was used to answer the questions. Subjects are professors and students of the computer science department; they were clustered in two groups: those with background knowledge on classification schemes and digital libraries visualization systems and those without this background.

The application of the pre- and posttests and the observation of user behavior during short sessions with the interface were useful to get the following results for the first group of users:

- The use of different colors allows users to easily identify the main categories.
- Users are familiar with two-dimensional conceptual representations, that is, representations that map information coming from the x- and y-axis.
- The icons formed with basic shapes (circle, square, and triangle) were considered appropriate.
- Learning to use this interface is easier and simpler in the first two levels than the tasks to access documents at the third level. These tasks require more practice.
- The organization of information seems logical, although visual clues as tooltip labels are recommended.

A different set of activities were carried out with the help of three additional students who participated as facilitators. They design some screen sketches (as an adaptation of a traditional storyboard technique) to illustrate and organize three different documents in the proposed interface. Some interesting results are the following ones: (1) the main elements were correctly identified and (2) the navigation scheme is understandable and simple. They suggest the incorporation of a map service, that is, that users are able to introduce a class name and the expected results were the respective code and vice versa.

We realize that a lot of effort is required in order to estimate the utility and usability of the proposed visualization scheme; however, we believe that preliminary results show positive clues of user satisfaction.

2.5 Conclusions

This chapter has presented SV, a visualization interface based on SVG charts for OAI records classified with the 1998 ACM CCS. The interface enables back-and-forth iteration with metadata. From basic construction to incorporation of simple behaviors, we have attempted to show users a high-level perspective of collections.

This work may help on the usability and design of user interfaces of small collections classified with CCS. We have tried to maintain the design of the SVG charts as independent as possible of the size of collections. We hope to overcome the restriction on the number of documents in a category by using visualization techniques such as fish-eye views.

As future work, we plan to incorporate a mechanism to extract automatically records from the ListRecords verb of OAI-PMH protocol in order to experiment with different collections as well as to add similarity information between documents.

References

1. Sánchez, J. A., Cervantes, O., Ramos, A., Medina, M. A., Lavariega, J., & Balam, E. (2011). Visualizing collaboration networks implicit in digital libraries using OntoStarFish. In *Proceedings of the 11th Annual International ACM/IEEE Joint Conference on Digital Libraries (JCDL)* (pp. 213–222). Available at http://dl.acm.org/citation?id=1998117.
2. Fung, B. C. M., Wang, K., & Ester, M. (2003). Hierarchical document clustering using frequent itemsets. In *Proceedings of the 3rd SIAM International Conference on Data Mining* (pp. 50–70). San Francisco: SDM.
3. Medina, M. A., & Sánchez, J. A. (2008). Ontoair: A method to construct lightweight ontologies from document collections. In *Proceedings of the Ninth Mexican International Conference on Computer Science* (pp. 11–25). Mexicali: ENC.
4. How to use the computer classification system. Association for Computer Machinery. Copyright 2013, ACM Inc. Available at http://www.acm.org/about/class/how-to-use.
5. Mirkin, B., Nascimento, S., & Moniz, L. (2008). Representing a computer science research organization on the ACM Computing Classification System. In *International Conference on Computer Science (ICCS Supplement '08)* (pp. 57–65). Available at http://ceur-ws.org/Vol-354/ p19.pdf.
6. Ginsburg, M. (2004). Visualizing research digital libraries with open standards. *Communications of the Association for Information systems, 13*, 336–358. http://aisel.aisnet.org/cais/vol13/ iss1/22/.
7. Cruz, M., Medina, M. A., Urbina, A. B., & Rodríguez, R. (2010 December). Mecanismo de navegación para colecciones de documentos digitales. Technical Report PII-25-08-10, Universidad Politécnica de Puebla, Ingeniería en Informática.
8. Martínez, A. L., Medina, M. A., Rodríguez, R., & Velázquez, J. (2010 December). Interfaz de navegación de colecciones de documentos organizados basada en SVG. Technical Report, Universidad Politécnica de Puebla, Ingeniería en Informática.
9. Hearst, M. (1999). User interfaces and visualization. In R. Baeza-Yates & B. Ribeiro-Neto (Eds.), *Modern information retrieval*. Boston: Addison-Wesley Longman.
10. Geroinmenko, V., & Chen, C. (2010). *Visualizing information using SVG and X3D. XML-based technologies for the XML- based web*. London: Springer.

Chapter 3
A Framework for the Improvement of Collaboration and Human-Computer-Human Interaction in Organizational Environments

Sergio López Antonaya, Crescencio Bravo Santos, and Jesús Gallardo Casero

Abstract The evolution of collaboration-related technologies opens new possibilities regarding the improvement of Human-Computer-Human Interaction processes and collective activities that occur within organizational environments. Part of the success of this improvement resides in the development of systems that equally fit the needs of both target organizations and end users. To meet these needs, it is necessary on the one hand to satisfy the requirements referred to intrinsic aspects of organizational structures and activities and to the diversity of skills and preferences observed in members of the organization itself on the other. For this reason, we introduce a framework based on the use of modeling and component composition techniques, which is intended to simplify the development of organizational collaborative systems, assisting developers in dealing with the requirements addressed above, and promote the involvement of end users in the software life cycle, by adding tailorability properties to final systems.

3.1 Introduction

The advancements achieved over the last few years in the fields of communications networks, computing devices, and web technologies have led society to a state of permanent connection, which in turn has facilitated the emergence of many new collaborative applications. The aforementioned technologies have also given rise

S. López Antonaya (✉) • C. Bravo Santos
Department of Information Technologies and Systems, University of Castilla-La Mancha, Paseo de la Universidad, 4, Ciudad Real 13071, Spain
e-mail: SLopezA@indra.es; Crescencio.Bravo@uclm.es

J. Gallardo Casero
Polytechnic School of Teruel, Department of Information Technologies and Systems, University of Zaragoza, Ciudad Escolar, s/n, Teruel 44003, Spain
e-mail: Jesus.Gallardo@unizar.es

V.M.R. Penichet et al. (eds.), *New Trends in Interaction, Virtual Reality and Modeling,*
Human-Computer Interaction Series, DOI 10.1007/978-1-4471-5445-7_3,
© Springer-Verlag London 2013

to new models of information systems or development paradigms which provide benefits not only to software professionals but also to end users who are now able to easily handle shared resources and workspaces [1]. Unfortunately, in formal organizational environments, the adoption of these technologies is generally more complicated for several reasons [2]. First of all, typical organizational structures that serve as a reference for establishing roles or policies of access to resources add an additional layer of complexity.

On the other hand, activities that take place in common organizations usually take the form of complicated business processes [3], involving numerous stakeholders, and are strongly associated with constraints of scope, time, and cost. Considering this context, it seems necessary to tackle the complex bidirectional integration of organizations and technologies, as well as to devise new ways for building more tailorable software [4].

For previous reasons, we propose a framework that pretends to overcome these difficulties and improve the support for usual Human-Computer-Human Interaction (HCHI) processes. The framework is revealed in the following sections, which are structured as indicated: Sect. 3.2 illustrates the current state of the art in the field of Computer-Supported Cooperative Work (CSCW) and related areas of study; Sect. 3.3 revises two relevant paradigms of major interest – Model-Driven Architecture (MDA) and Component-Based Development (CBD); Sect. 3.4 introduces the proposed framework; Sect. 3.5 illustrates a sample implementation of the framework; and, finally, Sect. 3.6 marks some conclusions and lines of work derived from present work.

3.2 State of the Art

Much of the work that has been done to date in the area of CSCW has been focused on the search for new mechanisms to enhance the traditional processes of communication, coordination, and cooperation [5]. However, in formal organizational environments, there are certain particularities that must be considered too, such as rigid organizational structures, complex business processes and workflows, and the heterogeneous skills and preferences exhibited by each member of the organization [6]. Most of the proposals formulated to date do not provide integrative perspectives for those questions, so it becomes necessary to review three conceptual areas that are quite relevant for our objectives: *Organizational Design*, *Business Processes and Workflows*, and *Groupware*.

3.2.1 *Organizational Design*

The field of *Organizational Design* is primarily focused on defining organizational structures that allow efficient management of processes and resources. In this sense, there are few works that address the relationship between the structure of organizations and the adoption of new technologies. Leifer [7] provides a review of organizational structures emerging as a result of the evolution of technology, such as *virtual organizations* or *adhocracies*. Penichet et al. [8] introduces some conceptual models that attach the domain of organizational structures to software development processes. The CIAM framework [9] includes social diagrams as part of its methodology. And finally, [4] affirms that one major objective of research in CSCW should be to integrate technology and organizations. In general, most studies reveal that the development of collaborative systems for organizational environments requires insight into the nature of organizations and the static elements that shape them [10].

3.2.2   Business Processes and Workflows

The areas of *Business Processes* and *Workflows* are dedicated to the study of new methods for structuring, organizing, and coordinating the different activities that take place within an organization and to build systems that provide adequate support for the satisfactory fulfillment of those activities. The importance of a good definition of business processes and workflows has been evaluated in [11], which states that the adoption of *Systems Workflow Management* (SGFTs) leads to higher productivity and faster response times in services offered and also that the use of technological systems to support the execution of workflows requires consideration of many organizational and social aspects. Moreover, much of the work conducted in the fields of business processes and workflows intends to provide formal or semiformal methods for describing workflows through models or notations. Thus, there exist many standards for the specification of business processes or workflows, such as *Business Process Management Notation* (BPMN) and *Workflow Management Facility* (WMF). From a more scientific perspective, some relevant works are *ConcurTaskTrees* (CTT) [12], especially indicated for the modeling of concurrent and interactive tasks, or *YAWL* [13] which is based in the application of *Petri Nets*. However, most of the proposals are not aimed at their application in the field of collaborative systems, which are characterized by a closer interaction level between humans and computers, and they require specification mechanisms that consider static and automatable aspects of business processes and the unpredictability of human behavior.

3.2.3   Groupware

The research field of *Groupware* is focused on the implementation of new technological tools that apply the theoretical results obtained in the area of *CSCW*, covering general issues such as the improvement of communication, coordination, and cooperation mechanisms, and some more specific others as the devising of new techniques for providing support to awareness or interaction processes. Regarding these points, much of the interest is dedicated to the handling of the variety of needs, skills, and preferences that each member of a collaborative group usually exhibits. Therefore, the need for tailorable systems in the area of *Groupware* is higher than in the case of traditional single-user software. Many works have followed this line, proposing tailorable system models based on the CBD paradigm: *CoCoWare.Net* platform [14] provides a set of components designed to provide different communication mechanisms that end users can combine. The *GroupKit* toolkit [15] contains several libraries that help to reduce the level of complexity of collaborative software development. Finally, the *EVOLVE* system [16] provides a component model that allows the composition of tailorable user interfaces. Nevertheless, despite all existing proposals, two problems remain: firstly, tailorability capacities have only been successfully implemented in the case of user interfaces and, secondly, instead, composition techniques have not reached an adequate level of flexibility that allows end users to freely adapt software systems.

3.3 Relevant Paradigms: Model-Driven Architecture and Component-Based Development

There are two paradigms that seem highly relevant for the fields of *Human-Computer-Human Interaction* and *Collaborative Systems*: *Model-Driven Architecture* (MDA) and *Component-Based Development* (CBD). On the one hand, the MDA paradigm appears to be one of the most promising solutions in order to adapt development processes to recent development trends, such as *Global Software Development* (GSD) [17], facilitating the participation of every stakeholder. In this sense, the MDA main value is given by the possibility of elaborating models that tackle with conceptual and technological aspects in an easily comprehensible way, even for nontechnical people. For these purposes, the MDA paradigm provides three types of models that are taken as reference in our framework: *Computation-Independent Models* (CIMs), which describe the domain of the problem to be resolved; *Platform-Independent Models* (PIMs), which collect the functionalities and constraints of the system that would be developed, although without deepen into technology issues; and *Platform-Specific Models* (PSMs), which attach aspects of the specific technology platform that will be used to deploy the system.

On the other hand, the CBD paradigm results in a very appropriate alternative when software is required to meet high levels of maintainability and reusability or when it is necessary to implement high-level specifications in heterogeneous technology platforms. Other advantages brought by this paradigm are as follows: helps to enroll end users in development processes; facilitates the incorporation of tailorability features to software products; helps to reduce the level of complexity by means of abstraction, encapsulation, and composition techniques; enhances the development of parallel and distributed software; and, finally, facilitates the creation of repositories of reusable components, what is particularly relevant when considering recent paradigms, such as Cloud Computing. For all these reasons, this paradigm also appears to be quite useful when used in conjunction with MDA foundations.

In resume, these two paradigms have been taken as reference for the specification of our framework in order to provide a solution that helps to meet the requirements that have been appointed in Sect. 3.2. The particular application of their principles will be explained in detail in following sections.

3.4   Framework Proposal

In this section we explain the fundamentals of our framework proposal, which is composed of three main parts: a *Conceptual Model* that describes the domain of organizational collaborative environments from an MDA perspective, a *Component Model* that takes the principles of CDB as reference and establishes a basis for the development of end-user tailorable collaborative systems, and, finally, a *Technology Architecture* that defines the technological requirements and guidelines that must be considered when implementing new organizational collaborative systems.

3.4.1   Conceptual Model

The *Conceptual Model* is intended to establish a flexible high-level semiformal reference from which to start the development of organizational collaborative environments. It is composed of three metamodels (defined in terms of UML class diagrams) related to the three previously addressed domains (*Organizational Design, Business Processes and Workflows*, and *Groupware*) to which we refer here as *Structure, Behavior*, and *Instrumentation* areas. Therefore, one of its main objectives is to establish a link with the CIM models defined in MDA paradigm.

3.4.1.1   Structure Metamodel

The *Structure* metamodel includes the necessary elements for modeling the static part of a collaborative organization, that is, those elements related to its existing internal structure and organizational roles. Although it is possible to find numerous types of nonhierarchical organizational structures in existing literature, such as *functional* or *geographical* ones, our metamodel has been formulated essentially thinking in a hierarchical scheme, which allows the subsequent association between the *Structure* and *Behavior* metamodels. This is considerably useful if common hierarchical decomposition procedures are taking into account for the specification of business processes and workflows.

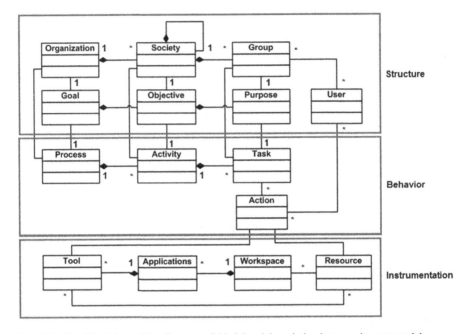

Fig. 3.1 Simplified view of the *Conceptual Model* and the relation between its metamodels

3.4.1.2   Behavior Metamodel

The *Behavior* metamodel provides the necessary elements to model the dynamic parts of an organization, namely, those elements related to business processes and workflows that are carried out. As in the case of the *Structure* metamodel, a hierarchical decomposition-oriented approach is preferable, since it provides two advantages: the first is that collaborative activities can be modeled in successive decreasing levels of abstraction until basic tasks can be assigned to end users or groups and the second is that the resulting models can be associated to different organizational units, so that the static and dynamic parts of the organization can be considered jointly.

3.4.1.3   Instrumentation Metamodel

The *Instrumentation* metamodel includes the necessary elements for modeling applications and tools that can be used by end users within their work environment. This last metamodel allows for performing composition activities following the CBD paradigm, since a work environment is devised as the conjunction of multiple workspaces (shared or not) which serve as hosts for different applications. In turn, these applications can be composed by a variable number of tools that make use of existing resources across the organizational structure, in order to help end users to achieve assigned tasks (Fig. 3.1).

3.4.2   Component Model

Our framework provides a *Component Model* (CM) that serves as reference for the elaboration of PIM and PSM equivalent models (as well as the *Conceptual Model* that serves as a reference for the elaboration of CIM equivalent models). Alike, this model helps to build two types of components: *Generic Components* (GC) that correspond to PIM models and help to solve some usual problems that appear when developing collaborative interactive systems or when development processes imply the use of MDA techniques and *Non-generic Components* (NGC) which correspond to PSM models and constitute the main resource for carrying out final software products implementation and deployment processes.

In particular, GCs provide solutions for next three important needs:

* A connection between high-level CIM models obtained from MDA initial modeling phases, with subsequent software units that must be developed and deployed.
* A notation that simplifies the incorporation of interaction and collaboration requirements to system specifications, without going into technical details but further facilitating its implementation in any technology platform.
* Development techniques that facilitate the inclusion of proper tailorability and reusability features into final systems.

Once GCs have been built, the final modeling process required to get functional systems consists in the conversion of GC components (PIM models) into NGC components. This process can be easily performed just by adding technology-dependent information to existing GCs. In fact, one way to do this could be as simple as embedding source code into GC components.

For further details of the foundations of the Component Model and its operational behavior, we provide an implementation in Sect. 3.5 and illustrate the global process in Fig. 3.2.

3.4.3   Technology Architecture

For completing the proposed framework, we have designed a *Technology Architecture*, so that after the sequential implementation of GC components from CIM models and GC components into NGC components, it is possible to deploy those resulting low-level components over a specific technology platform, in order to obtain a full functional organizational collaborative system. The three basic elements that constitute the proposed *Technology Architecture* are the *Communication Model*, the *Service Model*, and the *Runtime Model*.

3.4.3.1   Communication Model

The first component of the *Technology Architecture* is the *Communication Model*, which defines the notifications and events that must be handled by the underlying

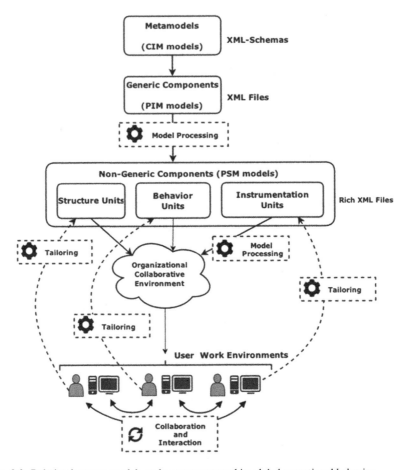

Fig. 3.2 Relation between models and components and its global operational behavior

system. This model specifies how the communication and collaboration processes between users must be conducted and how actions related to tailoring operations must be notified to every user, in order to correctly adapt every work environment. This Communication Model could be implemented using any existing communication scheme, for instance, *Client-Server*, *Distributed*, or *Hybrid* schemes could be used. However, it is important to notice that some widely accepted models such as *Service-Oriented Architecture* (SOA) may be more desirable than other options, due to the flexibility that they offer in order to modify or expand running systems.

3.4.3.2 Service Model

The *Service Model* defines the functions that the system must offer to developers and end users in order to facilitate maintainability, reusability, and tailorability. In this way, NGC components must be able to invoke high-level operations required by interactive and collaborative processes. Our framework introduces a solution based in the exposure of two specific interfaces for those specific types of process:

- *Interaction interface*: exposes functions that enable the access to resources located within the individual working environment (shared or not), in order to perform actions over them and obtain consequent responses.
- *Collaboration interface*: exposes functions that enable communication and collaboration processes between users and the access to shared resources located in other users' remote work environments.

In this way, it is possible to distinguish the two ways in which the functions defined in each of them can be invoked. The first one takes place when users perform a direct action against the elements located within their individual work environments. The second occurs when users participate in collaborative activities and their actions imply changes on the global shared environment.

3.4.3.3   Runtime Model

The last element of the proposed *Technology Architecture* is the *Runtime Model*, whose main objective is to provide the adequate support to modeling, development, and tailoring activities that can be performed by developers and end users. For this purpose, the *Runtime Model* must provide support for the next requirements:

- *Model processing*: a mechanism for parsing models must be supplied, so that it is possible to convert CIM models into PIM models and PIM models into PSM models. Depending on the final technology platform, it may be also necessary to provide auxiliary tools in order to run tasks such as source code generation and compilation or assembling of resulting software units.
- *Interaction and collaboration management*: the *Runtime Model* must provide access to the *Interaction and Collaboration Interfaces* exposed by the *Service Model*, as well as assume the management of technical problems such as conflicting states in shared artifacts or concurrency issues when collaborative workflows are being carried out (in collaboration with the *Service Model*).
- *Tailorability support*: it is necessary to rely on mechanisms that enable the handling of tailoring operations performed by users at runtime. From a technical point of view, this implies that deployed components must be able to explore and access the internal structure of the running system.

3.5   Framework Implementation

This section illustrates the feasibility of our framework in introducing a sample software platform that we have developed using Microsoft .NET technologies (although other common technologies, such as Java, could be used too). This platform implements certain tools that allow validating the advantages pursued by our framework, so in following points each component will be revised and its particular implementation described in an adequate level of detail.

3.5.1 Conceptual Model Implementation

The *Conceptual Model* described in Sect. 3.4.1 was initially defined in terms of UML class diagrams, although this is not an adequate computable format for the application of MDA techniques. For this reason, we have translated these graphical representations of the metamodels to *XML Schemas* format. This format facilitates the consequent modeling process of GC and NGC components and provides a higher level of maintainability and extensibility to own metamodels (thanks to the inherent characteristics of *XML* standards). In this manner, developers could extend the original metamodels to satisfy particular needs without affecting existing dependent models.

3.5.2 Generic Components Model Implementation

Once the metamodels have been translated to *XML Schemas*, the logical option for implementing GCs is by means of standard *XML Files*. By this approach, GCs can be elaborated by generating *XML Files* from previous *XML Schemas* or writing *XML Files* that can be validated against those same schemas. Another advantage of using *XML Files* is that end users can easily change their content (just editing internal sections) whenever they need to add or alter elements of the organizational environment or their own individual workspaces.

It must be remarked that, in the proposed implementation, there exists a difference between the components that are generated from XML Schemas corresponding to the areas of Structure and Behavior and those that are generated from XML Schemas associated to the area of Instrumentation: only the last ones are allowed to serve as basis for the generation of software components, since only this type of components allows the embedment of source code for the generation of tools and applications.

3.5.3 Technology Architecture Implementation

3.5.3.1 Communication Model

The first component of the *Technology Architecture*, the *Communication Model*, has been implemented by means of a hybrid communication scheme based on the exposure of *Web Services* facades (*Windows Communication Foundation* services) both in server and client machines, enabling a communication layer that helps to interconnect every machines in a highly flexible way. This schema also lets each individual machine to expose its own independent facade of *Web Services*, so that any user can develop new functions and serve them to the rest of the organizational environment, facilitating the modification of existing business processes and work-flows and the setting up of new ones.

3.5.3.2   Service Model

With regard to the Service Model, we have carried out the implementation of an *Application Programming Interface* (API) that simplifies the exposure of the *Interaction* and *Collaboration Interfaces* that were defined in Sect. 3.4.3.2. These interfaces encapsulate the complexities of underlying technologies and offer an appropriate level of abstraction that can be easily assimilated by both professional developers and end users without technical knowledge. In fact, calls to revealed functions can be embedded in concrete and delimited sections in NGCs, so it is possible for end users to reuse these portions of code from the *Rich XML Files* associated to NGCs.

3.5.3.3   Runtime Model

The implementation of the *Runtime Model* has required the development of a *Runtime Engine* whose main components are described below:

- *XML Files Parser*: parses the specifications contained by CIM, PIM, and PSM models, enabling the transformation of CIM models into software components.
- *Dynamic Source Code Generator*: generates native source code for the selected technology platform. In our case, we have used the *Code Document Object Model* (CodeDOM) technology, which automatically generates C# classes and methods.
- *Just-In-Time Compiler and Assembler*: compiles the source code provided by the *Dynamic Source Code Generator* and provides functional software units that the system can execute. This component allows tailoring the system with new functions that can be invoked during interaction processes between users and that may modify existing elements within the work environment.
- *User Interface Generator*: generates new user interfaces from the resulting elements that have been processed by the three previous components (Fig. 3.3).

3.6   Conclusions

In this work we have introduce a framework that pretends to facilitate a solution for three differentiated questions: simplify the development processes of organizational collaborative systems, improve the support for Human-Computer-Human

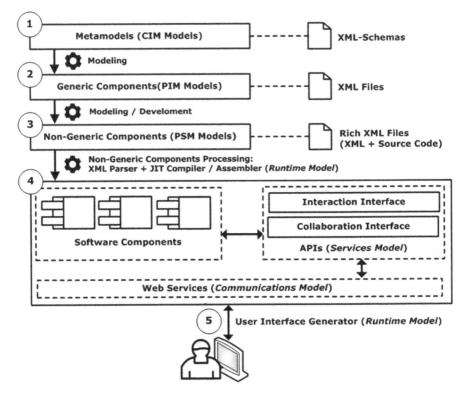

Fig. 3.3 *Technology Architecture* sample implementation and global functioning

Interaction in collaborative environments, and, at last, facilitate the inclusion of tailorable features in software products. This framework also aims to promote the enrollment of end users in the development process through an approach based on the combination of principles from the MDA and CBD paradigms.

With regard to future work, immediate objectives will center on the realization of several experiments with the purpose of empirically validating the advantages that our framework provides, discovering not contemplated disadvantages, and deepening the study of potential application scenarios.

Finally, we must remark that another promising line of work surges if we consider the Cloud Computing paradigm as one of the most valuables technological contexts for the implementations of collaborative technologies in formal organizations. In this sense, in the medium term, we will proceed to study the adaptation of the proposed framework to the particularities of Cloud-based environments.

References

1. Lieberman, H., Paternò, F., Klann, M., & Wulf, V. (2006). *End-user development: An emerging paradigm* (Human-computer interaction series, Vol. 9). Netherlands: Springer.
2. Antonaya, S. L., & Bravo, C. (2010). Towards a framework for the development of CSCW systems. In *Proceedings of the Seventh International Conference on Cooperative Design, Visualization and Engineering*. LNCS (Vol. 6240, pp. 117–120). Heidelberg: Springer.
3. Jing, Li. (2012). A location approach of sharing-resource in business collaboration system. In *Proceedings of the Second International Conference on Green Communications and Networks* (Vol. 1. LNCS, Vol. 223, pp. 607–613). Gandía (Valencia), Spain: Springer-Verlag Berlin Heidelberg.
4. Bannon, L. J., & Schmidt, K. (1989). CSCW: Four characters in search of a context. In *Proceedings of the First European Conference on Computer Supported Cooperative Work*(pp. 358–372). Gatwick, London: ACM Press.
5. Yankee Group: Communication, Collaboration, Coordination: The "Three Cs" of Workgroup Computing. (1995). *Yankee watch* (Vol. 3, No. 3).
6. Ackerman, M. S. (2000). The intellectual challenge of CSCW: The gap between social requirements and technical feasibility. *Journal of Computer-Human Interaction, 15*(2), 179–203.
7. Leifer, R. (1988). Matching computer-based information systems with organizational structures. *MIS Quarterly, 12*(1), 63–73.
8. Penichet, V., Lozano, M. D., & Gallud, J. A. (2006). Ontología para Estructuras Organizativas Colaborativas. In *Proceedings del VII Congreso Internacional de Interacción Persona Ordenador*. Universidad de Castilla – La Mancha. Puertollano, Spain.
9. Molina, A. I., Redondo, M. A., Ortega, M., & Hoppe, U. (2008). CIAM: A methodology for the development of groupware user interfaces. *Journal of Computer Science, 14*(9), 1435–1446.
10. Booth, P. (1991). Errors and theory in human-computer interaction. *Acta Psychologica, 78*, 69–96. Elsevier.
11. Kueng, P. (2000). The effects of workflow systems on organizations: A qualitative study. In *Business process management, models, techniques, and empirical studies* (LNCS, Vol. 1806, pp. 301–316). Springer-Verlag Berlin: Heidelberg.
12. Paternò, F., Mancini, C., & Meniconi, S. (1997). ConcurTaskTrees: A diagrammatic notation for specifying task models. In *Proceedings of the IFIP-TC13 International Conference on Human-Computer Interaction* (Vol. 96, pp. 362–369). London.
13. Van der Aalst, W. M. P., & ter Hofstede, A. H. M. (2005). YAWL: Yet another workflow language. *Journal of Information Systems, 30*(4), 254–275.
14. Slagter, R., Biemans, M., & ter Hofte, H. (2001). Evolution in use of groupware: Facilitating tailoring to the extreme. In *Proceedings of the Seventh International Workshop on Groupware*. (pp. 68–73). IEEE: Darmstadt, Germany.
15. Greenberg, S., & Roseman, M. (1996). Building real-time groupware with Groupkit, a groupware toolkit. *ACM Transactions on Computer-Human Interaction (TOCHI), 3*(1), 66–106.
16. Stiemerling, O., & Cremers, A. B. (2000). The EVOLVE project: Component-based tailorability for CSCW applications. *AI and Society, 14*, 120–141.
17. Vizcaino, A., García, F., Caballero, I., Villar, J. C., & Piattini, M. (2012). Towards an ontology for global software development. *IET Software, 6*(3), 214–225. IEEE.

Chapter 4
ORION: One More Step in Virtual Reality Interaction

Ernesto de la Rubia and Antonio Diaz-Estrella

Abstract This work presents the Orion project. It aims to create a low-cost virtual reality system that provides highly satisfying virtual experiences. To this end, the latest technology and the most significant findings from state-of-the-art research are applied to develop a system that provides natural interaction and full freedom of movement. The system's main features are as follows: wireless operation, real walking to navigate virtual environments, 3D gestural interaction, stereoscopic vision through a head-mounted display (HMD), and user movement tracking using inertial sensors. We discuss preliminary results and key aspects for developing the remainder of the project.

4.1 Introduction

To discuss virtual reality (VR) is to tell a story of *impressive experiences*, *disillusionment*, *significant challenges,* and *hope for the future*. The concept of VR is so fascinating that it could make true the dreams of most people. The primary issue is how to transform this concept into a system. At this point, numerous *challenges* arise; most of these challenges are related to the human senses and their excellent precision. The fact to face is that current technology is not able to feed our senses in the same manner as reality. Therefore, the expected *impressive experiences* are not impressive and expectations become *disillusionment*. Nevertheless, there is *hope for the future;* technological development is so quick that it seems clear that sooner or later our senses will be fed properly and then *impressive experiences* will be attained. Currently, we are progressing along this path towards the ultimate VR system. We think that we are not far from the inflection point at which sufficiently

E. de la Rubia (✉) • A. Diaz-Estrella
Department of Electronic Technology, University of Malaga, Malaga, Spain
e-mail: ernestodelarubia@uma.es; adiaz@uma.es

V.M.R. Penichet et al. (eds.), *New Trends in Interaction, Virtual Reality and Modeling*,
Human-Computer Interaction Series, DOI 10.1007/978-1-4471-5445-7_4,
© Springer-Verlag London 2013

satisfying experiences can be provided. In this chapter, we present the *Orion project*, which aims to go a step along the path towards this inflection point. Section 4.2 reviews the most relevant state-of-the-art findings regarding VR and current devices and trends. The *Orion project* is presented in Sect. 4.3. Finally, our conclusions can be found in Sect. 4.4.

4.2 Virtual Reality

Because of the multidisciplinary nature of VR, many different topics must be considered in this section. Most of the topics still pose challenges that are difficult to overcome. We will present these difficulties and describe the current approaches to address them.

Defining the concept of VR is not a straightforward task. This term is composed of two incompatible words. Nothing can be real and virtual simultaneously. Perhaps this contradiction makes this term attractive and interesting. Furthermore, virtual can be defined as being in essence or effect but not in fact. In return, defining what is reality leads to significant philosophical discussion. Aside from these difficulties, [1] provides this formal definition for VR: *a medium composed of interactive computer simulations that sense the participant's position and actions, providing synthetic feedback to one or more senses, giving the feeling of being immersed or being present in the simulation.*

Since the VR term was used for the first time in 1989 by Jaron Lanier, the founder of VPL Research [1], there have been several phases regarding the interest in VR (Fig. 4.1). According to [1], the first phase was the *Trigger* of the technology. Publicity and media contributed to significant interest in VR; this effect led to the second phase, *Peak of inflated expectations*. However, even currently, our expectations for sensory experiences in VR are not met [2]. Therefore, a *disillusionment* phase came in 1995. In this phase, the interest in VR reached low levels. However, as discussed before, the concept of VR is fascinating and relies on technology development to reach the point where sufficiently satisfying virtual experiences (VX) can be provided. Thus, research activity has continued since the *disillusionment* phase, and currently, the rapid technology development in handheld devices, high-resolution displays, wireless communication networks, tracking sensors, and computer graphics leads us to expect a second peak in the interest in the concept of VR. In fact, there are many hints that suggest a second peak: through a quick web search, it is easy to find recent blogs and white papers about VR with representative titles such as *How fast does "virtual reality" have to be to look like "actual reality"?*, *Hands On With The Oculus VR Rift*, *Virtual Reality's Greatest Hope*, and *Pushing Boundaries of Virtual Reality*. There are many other hints to expect this second peak in the interest in VR. HMD manufacturers are taking advantage of technological achievements regarding handheld devices. Now, low-cost HMDs with improved features can be built using mobile phone displays; this possibility has created huge

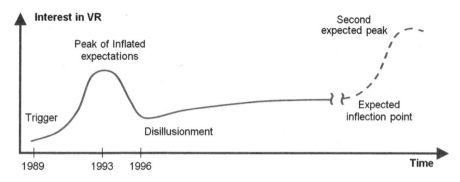

Fig. 4.1 Evolution of VR interest and expected trend

expectations.[1] It is clear that people love immersive and 3D interactive experiences. Tracking sensors as *Wii Remote* from *Nintendo* and *Kinect* from *Microsoft* are experiencing significant success. Recent developments and findings also support the hypothesis that the second peak is near; examples include the following: (a) the latest low-cost inertial sensors can reduce the overall system latency[2]; (b) wireless video transmission with high resolution and low latency intended for HMD is now possible[3]; (c) computer graphics achievements make it difficult to distinguish virtual environments (VE) from reality [2]; (d) the ray-tracing rendering technique, which significantly improves graphics quality, can now be performed in real time[4]; and (e) by applying the latest findings, it is possible to navigate through large VEs in the same manner as in real life (see below for further details). Additionally, there are studies that suggest the existence of this inflection point at which different aspects of VR systems will be sufficiently good [3–5].

4.2.1   *Immersion and Presence*

VR research activities require some means to evaluate experiments results. The concepts of immersion and presence are related to this purpose. According to [1],

---

[1]In 2012, Oculus VR, Inc., created a head-mounted display prototype that is called Oculus Rift. It is intended to revolutionize the manner in which people experience interactive content, and according to the tremendous expectations it has raised, the company will soon achieve this revolution. The project has garnered $2.4 million in funding from top video game companies and game enthusiasts around the world. Furthermore, they offered the Oculus Rift development kit (which cost $300) and expected hundreds of requests for it. They were overwhelmed when they received almost 10,000 requests (http://www.oculusvr.com).

[2]Oculus VR, Inc., is developing an inertial sensor that supports refresh rates as high as 1,000 Hz.

[3]Wireless video link from Sensics Inc. (http://sensics.com)

[4]Caustic Professional (https://caustic.com)

Immersion is the sensation of being in an environment. Within this concept, two different aspects can be considered: mental immersion and physical immersion. The first concept *refers to the feeling of being involved in the experience.* Even a book or a film can induce this feeling. The second concept comes from VR. We talk about *physical or sensory immersion when a system replaces or augments the stimulus to the participant's senses.*

The term *presence* or *sense of presence* is widely used by the VR community. According to [1], it is equivalent to mental immersion. It is the *feeling of being there* and plays an essential role in VR research because it helps evaluate the experiences of users in a VE. However, estimating the level of presence is as difficult as measuring a feeling. The most extended method to estimate the sense of presence is to provide a questionnaire to the participants after the experiment. Some of the most commonly used questionnaires are those proposed in [6, 7]. There are also other indirect methods to estimate the level of presence, such as monitoring some psychophysiological signals or observing the behavior of participants during the VX. Such methods are based, for instance, in the assumption that when the user feels immersed in the VE, his/her heart rate will increase in a dangerous situation or he/she will dodge a virtual object that is going to hit him/her. These methods have a disadvantage: they impose limitations during the design process of the VX. Many studies have been conducted to find methods to improve VXs to increase the sense of presence. Such methods include the following: display and animate the avatar of the user [8], walk to navigate the VE (exactly as in reality) [8], play footstep sounds while walking [9], and start the VX in a VE that mimics the real lab (transitional environments) [10]. Chertoff, Goldiez, and LaViola [11] reference 86 studies in which different aspects of the VR system are evaluated through the self-reported level of presence; such measures include tracking level, stereoscopic vision, image quality, field of view (FOV), sound quality, etc. However, it is necessary to be aware that estimating the level of presence is far from accurate; for instance, sometimes the behavior of participants contradicts their verbally reported presence. Sherman and Craig [1] relate how a participant who claimed not to feel immersed in the VE tried to lean on the virtual furniture when he was asked to stand up. In addition, [12] applied their own proposed questionnaire in addition to that from Witmer and Singer to compare the level of presence in a VX and in its real equivalent. The results demonstrate that both questionnaires cannot pass the *reality test* because they reported no significant differences between the VX and the real world. This is one of the reasons that alternative procedures to self-report presence have been sought. For instance, [11] proposes a method to evaluate a VX that is based on elements from experimental design, such as sensory, cognitive, affective, active, and relational.

4.2.2 Significant Findings and Involved Technologies

There are several new technologies of interest for VR systems. This section reviews some of the technologies that are related to interaction, sensory feedback, graphical realism, and contents.

Interaction plays an essential role in VXs. Currently, users find difficult to precisely manipulate virtual objects. Thus, much work remains to be performed, and it is easy to find recent studies about interaction design and methodology [13]. VR systems require interaction techniques to navigate, manipulate, and communicate. For this purpose, user body movements, pose, gaze, voice, etc. are used if natural interaction is required. There are many tracking technologies (e.g., optical, electromagnetic, ultrasound, and inertial) to capture the position or orientation of a user's body. Of all of the techniques, inertial sensors are unique because they do not require a supporting infrastructure that provides references; instead, they use gravity and the magnetic field of the Earth. Thus, by using inertial sensors, the tracking area can be larger and the system cost can be reduced. The major drawback of inertial sensors is that position estimation is strongly affected by drift errors because position is obtained by a double integration of acceleration; hence, small errors are accumulated in the estimated velocity. However, orientation can be measured without drift errors. Inertial sensors are composed of a 3-axis gyroscope, a 3-axis accelerometer, and a 3-axis magnetometer. Kalman filtering is often used in data fusion algorithms to estimate orientation and position [14]. There are several motion capture (MOCAP) systems to track full-body movements. Optical approaches employ several cameras and apply image processing to track points in the tracking area.[5] Otherwise, inertial MOCAP systems measure orientation using inertial sensors.[6] The optical approach is more accurate, but the tracking area is limited. Inertial systems do not suffer from this problem because they do not relay on an external infrastructure to provide references. Optical MOCAPs are very well suited to determine how accurate the position estimation from an inertial tracker is. This crosscheck could be used to study and reduce drift errors from a single inertial tracker in a gesture-interaction system.

There are many techniques for navigating VEs [15]. Some studies suggest that *real walking* (RW) is the best method [8]. This technique lets the user walk in the VE exactly as he/she does in the real world. However, RW has an important disadvantage; the real workspace must be slightly larger than the VE. Redirection methods can ease these restrictions by manipulating the position and orientation of the point of view. This manipulation is performed to keep the user away from the real walls in such a manner that he/she cannot notice the manipulation [16]. Additionally, virtual elements called distractors can be included in the VE to attract the user's attention while redirection is being performed [17]; this method is used to increase the redirection's extent. In addition, [18] proposes a complementary method to deal with the boundaries of the workspace: considering impossible spaces, such as self-overlapping architectural layouts, they found that virtual rooms may overlap as much as 56 % before the user notices the overlap. As a last resort, resetting techniques [19], which disrupt the VX to modify the correspondence between the real and virtual world, can also be applied. By resetting, the user is again kept

---

[5]NaturalPoint, Inc. (http://www.naturalpoint.com)

[6]XSens. (http://www.xsens.com)

away from the wall, but in this case, he/she is aware of the changes in the VE. Furthermore, it is good practice to prevent the user from thinking of real walls during the VX. To achieve this, his/her eyes can be covered while he/she enters the room in which the VX will take place. Transitional environments could also be used for this purpose [10].

Regarding selection and manipulation in VEs, several methods can be considered [1]. Among them, gestural interfaces that mimic real-world interaction (*direct control*) seem to be the most suitable for natural interaction. Instrumented gloves and body trackers have been used for this purpose. In particular, inertial sensors attached to the hands could be an interesting starting point to design a low-cost RW VR system. However, as mentioned above, using inertial sensors leads to drift errors in position. An inertial MOCAP can address this problem by considering relative orientation among the different parts of the body. In return, when a single tracker is attached to each hand to perform manipulation and selection, the position error will increase over time from the last steady state. In this case, it is useful to be aware of the dominance of vision over proprioception [20] because certain errors can be admitted. Another challenging task is to select and release virtual objects. Choumane, Casiez, and Grisoni [21] propose a method to accomplish this by processing the hand trajectory. Moreover, gesture recognition using inertial sensors attached to the hands could be an interesting starting point to design an inertial interaction paradigm that could be the best approach to create an RW VR system.

Sensory feedback is essential to achieve good physical immersion. This feedback includes several modalities, such as visual, aural, haptic, etc. Visual feedback is the most important and still faces many challenges. Aural feedback could be considered resolved through the use of 3D sound.[7] Haptic feedback is very desirable but currently difficult and costly to implement.

An HMD not only provides visual feedback but also can include aural feedback and inputs such as voice interaction or more advanced features such as gaze tracking. The HMD is an essential element in VR because the sense of sight provides a large quantity of information. The major issue to overcome to design HMDs is the outstanding performance of the human eye. Our FOV is greater than 180° horizontally and approximately 120° vertically. The human visual acuity is approximately 0.01°. Therefore, if we assume that a pixel corresponds to this visual acuity, a perfect HMD would provide resolution of $18,000 \times 12,000$ pixels and a field of view of 180° horizontally and 120° vertically. Current technology is still far from achieving these specifications. Boger [3] conducted a survey among VR experts and users. He obtained the minimum features of a good enough HMD: an FOV of $120 \times 50°$, resolution of at least $1,600 \times 1,200$ pixels, and mass of no more than 250 g. Current HMDs are approaching some of these specifications.[8] Moreover, the cables of HMDs significantly harm the VX quality [8]. However, recently, there are commercial wireless systems that transmit high-resolution video with very low

---

[7]3D sound is based on HRTFs (head-related transfer functions).

[8]Oculus Rift features: field of view: 110° diagonal, 90° horizontal. Resolution: $1,280 \times 800$ (640×800 per eye). Mass: 220 g (http://www.oculusvr.com)

latency and are intended to be used with HMD.[9] Latency is another key aspect of HMDs. Latency is the delay from when the head orientation is measured until the instant at which the corresponding image is displayed to the user. Latency errors can be approximately 3° in current systems.[10] di Luca [22] proposes a method to measure the latency in VR systems, and currently, commercial systems are beginning to measure latency.[11]

Another key aspect for improving VX is the graphical realism. Modern computer graphics techniques can create high-quality VEs and have the potential to generate real-time images that will be indistinguishable from reality. The emergence of specific hardware to render ray-traced images in real time supports this idea.[12] There are many graphic engines that can be used to create VEs. Some are commercial products such as the *Crysis Engine*, the *Unreal Engine*, and *Unity 3D*. Others can be used freely; examples include *Ogre3D*, *Horde3D*, and the *Blender game engine*. Most of the games engines are intended to develop games, but there are also specific tools to create VR applications, such as *LinceoVR* and *3DVia Virtools*.

Designing VX aspects such as the context, the contents, and the manner in which the action occurs has a huge importance to make the user forget about the real world and helps him/her to be fully involved in the VE [2]. Chertoff, Goldiez, and LaViola [11] consider the design of the VX, including affective and cognitive factors. They propose a test to evaluate holistic VXs, and their results demonstrate that presence is increased significantly when these factors are applied to the VX design process.

In summary, the presented findings and technologies can establish the basis for the development of a VR system with natural interaction and full freedom of movement. This idea motivates the Orion project.

4.3   Orion Project

The Orion project[13] aims to create a VR system that provides highly satisfying VXs. It arises from an on-going PhD thesis to study the following hypotheses:

- *H1: A second peak in the interest in VR will arise within the next 6 years.*
- *H2: It is possible to create a VR system based on five inertial sensors that will be able to provide RW, gestural interaction, and full freedom of movement without using external references.*

---

[9] http://sensics.com/products/low-latency-hd1080-wireless-video

[10] When the users turns his/her head at 60° per second and uses an HMD with 100° of horizontal FOV and 1280 pixels of horizontal resolution, and the overall latency is 50 milliseconds, then the displayed image is shifted 3° or, equivalently, 35 pixels.

[11] Oculus Latency Tester (http://www.oculusvr.com)

[12] Caustic Ray-Tracing Accelerator Boards (https://caustic.com)

[13] On the project website can be found the research results, the used resources, videos from the prototypes, and developed applications [23].

- *H3: The cost of the system will decrease below 2000€ within the next 6 years.*
- *H4: This system will be able to provide sufficiently satisfying VXs that the user will evaluate through the most used questionnaires in RV research.*

H1 could be verified by estimating the turnover related to the VR market or the investment volume in VR over the years. H1 motivates this project, but verifying the hypothesis is beyond the project's objectives. To test H2 and H3, we are designing and building several prototypes of VR systems [23, 24]. To verify H4, we will conduct a user study once the system is ready. Furthermore, we find it interesting to evaluate the connection between H1 and H4 by asking questions such as the following: If this system were commercially available, would you be interested in buying it? How much are you willing to pay for it? From 0 to 10, how important do you think investments in VR are?

To start working, it is necessary to consider objectives and tasks to fulfill the requirements of the Orion project:

Interaction: *Create an interactive VR system with full freedom of movement.*

Task: Implement the real-walking navigation technique using inertial sensors.
Task: Create a gestural interaction paradigm using inertial tracking.

Presence: *Achieve a high presence level in the user tests.*

Task: Identify relevant findings from the state-of-the-art research related with the project.
Task: Integrate the obtained key findings into the system.
Task: Carefully design the VX to involve the user.

Sensory Immersion: *Feed the senses of the user properly and keep the system cost affordable.*

Task: Compare the latest devices and select those that are most suitable for the project.
Task: Create photorealistic VEs.

Main Objective: *Develop a VR system that provides a highly satisfying VX.*

In the remainder of this section, the main components of the proposed system are described, the advances in RW and inertial hand tracking are explained, and finally, the tools developed and the VEs created to test prototypes are presented.

4.3.1 System Description

To mimic reality, we decided to design a VR system that provides full freedom of movement. To do so, the best navigation technique, RW, must be applied. This decision implies using an HMD and tracking the movements of the user in a large area. To minimize the cost of the system, we decided to use inertial sensors and

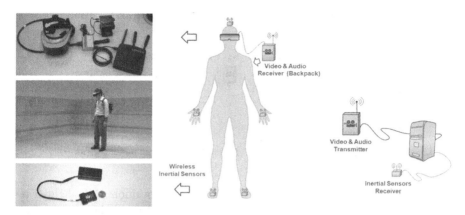

Fig. 4.2 Prototype components: HMD, wireless video link, wireless inertial sensors, and PC

face the challenge of treating drift errors and the absence of absolute references. We added gestural interaction to improve the user experience. We decided to use five wireless inertial sensors placed on the head, feet, and hands to track the movements of the user. Using the minimum number of sensors reduces the cost, while wearing the VR system is more comfortable. To animate the avatar of the user, inverse kinematic techniques can be employed. Finally, a computer and two wireless video transmission modules complete the list of components of the system. Figure 4.2 presents these components.[14] Signals from inertial sensors are sent to the computer, where they are processed to estimate the position and orientation of head, feet, and hands. Then, a stereo rendering of the VE is performed. This rendering and the corresponding 3D audio stream are sent to the receiver module and finally delivered to the HMD.

According to the state-of-the-art research, two challenging tasks arise from the proposed approach. The first task is to implement the real-walking navigation technique using inertial sensors. The second task is tracking the hands to interact with the VE while addressing significant drift errors in position.

4.3.2   Real-Walking Navigation Technique Using Inertial Sensors

At this point, we aim to estimate the position and orientation of the head from three inertial sensors placed on the head and feet. Obtaining the head orientation is quite simple because there are many libraries and algorithms that perform the required

---

[14]We have used wireless Inertia Cube 3 inertial sensors from Intersense (www.intersense.com), the zSight HMD from Sensics (http://sensics.com), and its wireless video link.

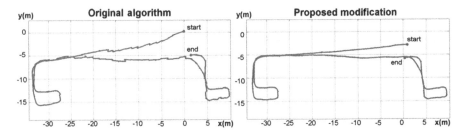

Fig. 4.3 Accuracy improvement in estimated foot trajectories using an inertial sensor

data fusion. The challenging task is to estimate the head position while the user is walking. To the best of our knowledge, this difficulty has not yet been overcome. Because of the lack of absolute references, the current position must be derived from the previous position (dead reckoning). Thus, we must address position drift errors. We estimate the head position from the positions of the feet; thus, the first task is to derive the foot position from inertial signals. To do so, a double integration of acceleration must be performed, but this integration is not a straightforward task. The acceleration provided by the sensor must be transformed from the sensor coordinate system to the earth coordinate system; then, the gravity component must be subtracted. The obtained acceleration is due to the foot movement, and this is the acceleration that we must integrate twice. To perform the aforementioned coordinate system transformation, the orientation of the sensor must be known. Once the acceleration is integrated twice, a drift error in the estimated velocity appears during each step. At the end of the step when the foot is steady on the floor, the velocity can be reset and the previous estimations of position can be corrected; this correction is called *zero-velocity update* (ZUPT) [14]. This entire process can be performed by applying pedestrian dead reckoning algorithms. We use the algorithm proposed in [14], which uses Kalman filtering to improve the estimation by reducing the effects of noise in the signals. However, there is still an issue to overcome: the corrections due to the ZUPT are too abrupt. This abruptness could lead to unexpected changes in the estimated head position. We have improved this algorithm to reduce the correction length [25]. Now, the position estimation is valid for longer. The same idea can be applied to improve the tracking of the hands. Figure 4.3 shows this improvement in an estimated path that is approximately 140 m in length.

Once the position estimation is sufficiently accurate, it can be displayed and animated using one of the tools developed in the project, the *Inertial Signal Analyser*. A sample track in which the user is climbing stairs is shown in Fig. 4.4.

The next task to accomplish is estimating the head position from the estimated positions of the feet. To do so, we use biomechanics models of the human gait. Furthermore, we use an optical MOCAP system[15] that has millimeter accuracy to

---

[15]NaturalPoint, Inc. (http://www.naturalpoint.com)

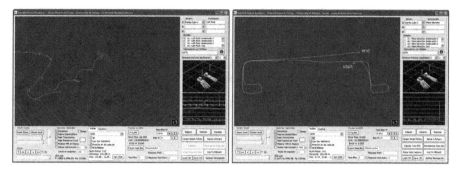

Fig. 4.4 The Signal Analyser animates the shoe of the user and displays its trajectory

compare feet positions with those obtained from the inertial sensors. This approach is also useful to derive the head position from the feet positions. Finally, we must address the limits of the real room in which the VX takes place. The drift error in position requires us to increment the security margins to avoid collisions with the walls. However, we can use redirect walking techniques [16], distractors [17], or impossible spaces [18] to relax this restriction. Furthermore, resetting techniques [19] could be employed as a last resort.

4.3.3   Inertial Hand Tracking

Tracking the orientation and position of the hands using inertial sensors is another challenging goal because of the significant drift errors in position. To the best of our knowledge, a sufficiently satisfying solution has not yet been found. In this case, the same ideas and principles as used in the inertial tracking of the feet can be applied, and again, obtaining the orientation is not a problem. To overcome the drift errors in position, we propose a *rapid interaction paradigm* in which the user must perform round-trip movements that should last less than 2 s. We have obtained promising results in preliminary tests. The *Inertial Signal Analyser* presents examples of tracked trajectories in Fig. 4.5.

The initial position of the hand must be near the body and approximately 10 cm above the hips. To improve the tracking accuracy, we use the technique proposed in [25] and we also apply guidance algorithms when the hand approaches the initial position. We think this approach is very well suited to interaction in VEs. For instance, using round-trip movements, a virtual button can be pressed or a door can be opened; furthermore, circular movements can be employed to rotate an object in any direction or to perform sliding operations in a virtual interface. In addition, the technique proposed in [21] is quite interesting for picking virtual objects for manipulation and releasing them.

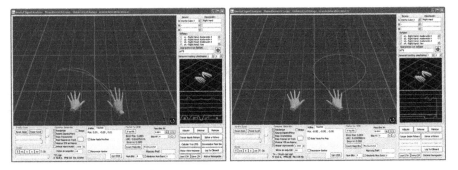

Fig. 4.5 The Signal Analyser animates the hand of the user and displays its trajectory

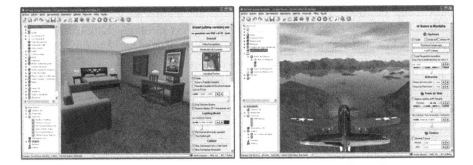

Fig. 4.6 VSD interface: room in virtual hotel and Wii Remote-controlled flight simulator

4.3.4 Developed Tools

To accomplish the objectives of this project, several tools have been developed.[16] We have created a *tool generator for an interaction lab* [26] to address custom developments derived from the research activity. It is composed of an application to design interactive VEs that is called the *Virtual Scene Designer* (VSD) and a software development kit (SDK). Figure 4.6 presents the VSD interface.

Among its main features, we highlight the following: HMD support; inertial sensor support; 3D stereo modes; 3D sound using OpenAL; navigators: walk (HMD, keyboard, mouse, and Wiimote) and fly (keyboard and Wiimote); Kinect sensor support; an integrated development environment for GLSL shaders; dynamic reflection; textures from videos or webcams; antialiasing; motion blur; particles, occlusion queries, and planar shadows. Designing VEs and interactive animations can be accomplished quickly using the VSD. Additionally, the VSD works together with an SDK that is intended to develop custom applications. This SDK takes

---

[16]These tools and videos that show them working can be found at the project web site [23].

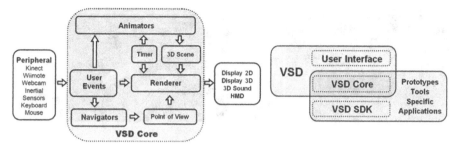

Fig. 4.7 VSD internal scheme and its relation with the VSD application and its SDK

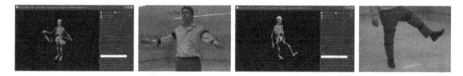

Fig. 4.8 Real-time tracking and animation of arms and legs using inertial motion capture

advantage of the VEs and interactive animations designed with the VSD. Thus, this approach is very well suited for developing custom applications quickly because general aspects are modelled through a user interface, and specific issues are modelled using a programming language. Figure 4.7 presents schemes from the VSD and its SDK. According to the project's objectives, we have used the VSD and its SDK to create several tools that are discussed below.

The *MOCAP Tool* is our first attempt to create a real-walking VR system in the Orion project. It tracks the orientation of the legs and arms. We abandoned this idea to improve the ergonomic aspects of the system and to reduce its cost. However, the system is very well suited for gestural interaction; for instance, the user can draw 3D lines in the air. Figure 4.8 shows its interface.

The *inertial signal analyser* takes information from the inertial sensors and assists in the process of understanding the manner in which the inertial signals behave. The final purpose is to help researchers develop new tracking algorithms. Currently, the analyser includes some of the techniques presented in previous sections. Figure 4.9 shows its interface under different working modes.

The *point-of-view analyser* has been created to evaluate the RW prototypes developed in the Orion project. It is able to display and animate the avatars of the participants. Rotations of the head and the body are also displayed in addition to the followed tracks. It is also possible to select a participant and reproduce exactly what he/she observed during the experiment. Figure 4.10 shows this tool.

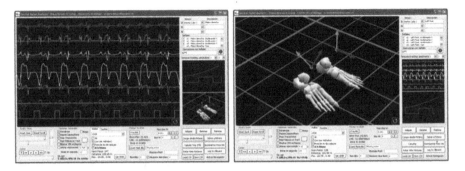

Fig. 4.9 Inertial signal analyser animating 2D signals and 3D vectors from inertial sensors

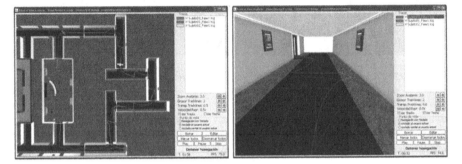

Fig. 4.10 Point-of-view analyser animating avatars of participants after an experiment

4.3.5 Virtual Environments to Test Prototypes

To test the developed prototypes, we created three VEs. The first one is the *iHotel*, in which the user can visit a hall, a courtyard, a room, and a painting gallery. In the room, the user can manipulate virtual interfaces to control lights, radio, TV, etc. The idea behind the second and third VEs is related to that presented in [18]. We can take advantage of VR's nature to improve the VX in a limited physical area. An endless corridor is changed when the user cannot notice the change to guide him/her through an incomprehensible path with no alternative choice. The third VE is a preliminary version of an interactive museum. It is composed of square rooms that also change when the user cannot notice the change. This idea provides a method to offer the user a countless number of different VX while he/she is within a limited physical workspace. Figure 4.11 shows these VEs.

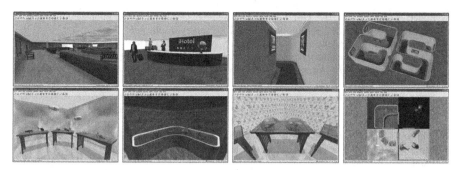

Fig. 4.11 3D scenes: iHotel (*upper-left*), corridor (*upper-right*), virtual museum (*bottom*)

4.4 Conclusions

We have discussed the key aspects of VR, its evolution and trends that lead us to expect a second period of success in VR. We think that we are not far from this second period, and we aim to create a prototype of a VR system that provides highly satisfying VXs. This is the main goal of the Orion project that we have presented in this work. We have discussed preliminary results, and further key aspects for accomplishing the development of the rest of the project have also been discussed. Our prototype is not the ultimate solution. For example, it does not stimulate the senses of touch, taste, or smell because of technological limitations. Furthermore, there are some specific movements, such as jumping, that the tracking system cannot detect because of reasons with the ergonomics and also the objective of obtaining a low-cost system. Nevertheless, the system proposed advances in VR interaction by providing RW and eliminating cables and restrictions on the walking space. These advancements together with suitable design of the VX will most likely improve the sense of presence and allow for new and exciting applications for videogames, walkthrough VEs, and virtual communities.

Acknowledgments This research has been partially supported by the Junta de Andalucia and the project CENIT España Virtual, within the Ingenio 2010 program, subcontracted by Elecnor Deimos.

References

1. Sherman, W. R., & Craig, A. B. (2003). *Understanding virtual reality: Interface, application, and design.* San Francisco, CA: Morgan Kaufmann.
2. Lindeman, R.W., & Beckhaus, S. (2009). Crafting memorable VR experiences using experiential fidelity. In *ACM Symposium on Virtual Reality Software and Technology, VRST* (pp. 187–190). Virginia: USA.

3. Boger, Y. (2008). The 2008 HMD survey: are we there yet? White paper published by Sensics Inc. http://www.sensics.com/files/documents/2008SurveyResults.pdf
4. Cummings, J. J., Bailenson, J. N., & Fidler, M. J. (2012). How immersive is enough? A foundation for a meta-analysis of the effect of immersive technology on measured presence. In *Proceedings of the International Society for Presence Research Annual Conference*. Philadelphia: USA.
5. Stone, R. (2009). Serious games: Virtual reality's second coming? *Virtual Reality, 13*(1), 1–2.
6. Slater, M., Usoh, M., & Steed, A. (1994). Depth of presence in virtual environments. *Presence: Teleoperators and Virtual Environments, 3*, 130–144.
7. Witmer, B. G., & Singer, M. J. (1998). Measuring presence in virtual environments: A presence questionnaire. *Presence: Teleoperators and Virtual Environments, 7*(3), 225–240.
8. Usoh, M., Arthur, K., & Whitton, M. C. et al. (1999). Walking, walking-in-place, flying in virtual environments. In *Proceedings Conference on Computer Graphics and Interactive Techniques* (pp. 359–364). Los Angeles: USA.
9. Nordahl, R. (2005). Self-induced footsteps sounds in virtual reality: Latency, recognition, quality and presence. In *Proceedings of the 8th Annual Workshop on Presence* (pp. 353–354). London: United Kingdom.
10. Steinicke, F., Bruder, G., Hinrichs, K., Steed, A., & Gerlach, A. L. (2009). Does a gradual transition to the virtual world increase presence? In *Proceedings – IEEE Virtual Reality* (pp. 203–210). Louisiana: USA.
11. Chertoff, D. B., Goldiez, B., & LaViola, Jr. J. J. (2010). Virtual experience test: A virtual environment evaluation questionnaire. In: *Proceedings – IEEE Virtual Reality* (pp. 103–110). Massachusetts: USA.
12. Usoh, M., Catena, E., Arman, S., & Slater, M. (2000). Using presence questionnaires in reality. *Presence: Teleoperators and Virtual Environments, 9*(5), 497–503.
13. Frees, S. (2010). Context-driven interaction in immersive virtual environments. *Virtual Reality, 14*(4), 277–290.
14. Fischer, C., Sukumar, P. T., & Hazas, M. (2012). Tutorial: Implementation of a pedestrian tracker using foot-mounted inertial sensors. *IEEE Pervasive Computing, 12*, 17–27.
15. Craig, A. B., Sherman, W. R., & Will, J. D. (2012). *Developing virtual reality applications: Foundations of effective design*. San Francisco, CA: Morgan Kaufmann.
16. Steinicke, F., Bruder, G., Jerald, J., et al. (2010). Estimation of detection thresholds for redirected walking techniques. *IEEE Transactions on Visualization and Computer Graphics, 16*(1), 17–27.
17. Peck, T. C., Fuchs, H., & Whitton, M. C. (2012). The design and evaluation of a large-scale real-walking locomotion interface. *IEEE Transactions on Visualization and Computer Graphics, 18*(7), 1053–1067.
18. Suma, E. A., Lipps, Z., Finkelstein, S., et al. (2012). Impossible spaces: Maximizing natural walking in virtual environments with self-overlapping architecture. *IEEE Transactions on Visualization and Computer Graphics, 18*(4), 555–564.
19. Williams, B., Narasimham, G., & Rump, B. et al. (2007). Exploring large virtual environments with an HMD when physical space is limited. In *ACM International Conference Proceeding Series* (pp. 41–48).
20. Burns, E., Whitton, M. C., & Razzaque, S. et al. (2005). The hand is slower than the eye: A quantitative exploration of visual dominance over proprioception. In *Proceedings of IEEE Virtual Reality* (pp. 3–10). Bonn: Germany.
21. Choumane, A., Casiez, G., & Grisoni, L. (2010). Buttonless clicking: Intuitive select and pick-release through gesture analysis. In *Proceedings – IEEE Virtual Reality* (pp. 67–70). Massachusetts: USA.
22. di Luca, M. (2010). New method to measure end-to-end delay of virtual reality. *Presence: Teleoperators and Virtual Environments, 19*(6), 569–584.
23. Orion project. (2012). Retrieved March 9, 2013, from http://www.diana.uma.es/orion/eIndex.html

24. de la Rubia, E., & Diaz-Estrella, A. (2012). A forward step in virtual reality. In *Proceedings of IADIS CGVCVIP 2012 Conference Lisbon* (pp. 171–174). Portugal.
25. de la Rubia, E., & Diaz-Estrella, A. (2013). Improved pedestrian tracking through Kalman covariance error selective reset. *Electronic Letters, 49*(7), 464–465.
26. de la Rubia, E., & Diaz-Estrella, A. (2012). Tool generator for an interaction lab. In *INTERACCION '12: Proceedings of the 13th International Conference on Interacción Persona-Ordenador* (pp. 285–288). Elche: Spain.

Chapter 5
Towards the Commodification of Augmented Reality: Tools and Platforms

Hector Olmedo and Jorge Augusto

Abstract The design and development of products based on or related to Augmented Reality (AR) and Mixed Reality (MR) has boomed in recent years, due not only to a growing market interest but to the technical ease and low cost of the many available tools. This chapter introduces the most popular hardware and software tools and technologies to develop AR and MR applications, in order to serve as starting point to anyone interested in developing such systems. Elements needed to develop AR/MR will be presented objectively, and some example projects will be described.

5.1 Introduction

The AR concept involves the combination of several technologies in order to mix computer-generated objects with real-time video streaming [1]. MR is halfway between AR and VR, as it deals with the different levels of contribution from each of these domains in one video output [2]. So it is in the context of the MR where certain techniques, such as using physical objects from the user's visual environment as interaction elements with the virtual world, make sense. The potential of techniques related to AR/MR is not completely explored yet, and it is done slowly due to needs of specific hardware devices. But nowadays, data can be taken from a cam or GPS with an average computer or smartphone. Even projects like Google Glass [3], which could be considered as "wearable computing," are AR related. This chapter

H. Olmedo (✉)
Universidad de Valladolid, Valladolid, Spain

Universidad Rey Juan Carlos, Madrid, Spain
e-mail: holmedor@gmail.com

J. Augusto
Universidad Rey Juan Carlos, Madrid, Spain
e-mail: jorgeaug@gmail.com

V.M.R. Penichet et al. (eds.), *New Trends in Interaction, Virtual Reality and Modeling*,
Human-Computer Interaction Series, DOI 10.1007/978-1-4471-5445-7_5,
© Springer-Verlag London 2013

introduces involved technologies and also lists and describes the most popular hardware/software AR/MR tools and their main features. Common applications will be reviewed too by listing some example projects. Finally, conclusions will be exposed.

5.2 Technologies

In order to have a global vision of the involved technologies, a review of the most used ones will be detailed, based on [4].

5.2.1 Computer Vision

The potential of computer vision technologies is based in the ability of taking advantage of the visual characteristics of the environment, naturally taken by a camera. Its advantages are that modifying the environment is not a requirement and that there are no limitations like with magnetic, mechanical, or ultrasound devices. It is the only technology capable of guaranteeing the alignment between real and virtual world with a precision of pixels because it is based on them [5]. Two main techniques are considered:

- Marker Systems are systems based in printed reference patterns, as the ones described in [6] for AR Tennis. These patterns provide easy to recognize references to AR/MR systems. The use of printed markers implies slight modifications of the environment, but it has been, in fact, the easiest way to make several projects work.
- Markerless Systems are systems based in patterns found on the raw image through the use of computer vision techniques. They are able to create environments referencing recognizable characteristics from the video output, like facial features, gesture parameters, or any kind of findable patterns in known environments without the need of using printed markers. The image processing algorithms will be more complex than in the case of marker systems.

5.2.2 Tracking and Geolocation

Video can be annotated and labeled thanks to the ability of the user device (mostly smartphones) to detect its own orientation and position by means of the use of sensors like GPS, magnetometers, and accelerometers or data obtained from the phone radio network [7].

5.2.3 Visualization

Either interacting with a real world with more information showed to the users (AR) or interacting with a new reality based on the real world (MR), there is a need of different devices that can be classified as follows:

- Projector based: for more than one user sharing the AR/MR environment
- Head-mounted displays: for a single user, thus enjoying a better feeling of immersion
- Onboard systems: embedded on a car dashboard, for example
- Browser-based systems: applications that run on computers and mobile devices such as smartphones, tablets, or laptops that are able to overlay synthetic images or user controls over the video captured by the device's camera

The graphic engines needed to animate the artificial objects that "augment" the real world, like JMonkeyEngine [8], or Open Wonderland [9], used to build new realities, deserve special mention. These technologies, combined with the keyboard- and mouse-based classical graphical interaction, provide new methods of communication with the AR/MR worlds developed. Next, a list of several hardware and software tools for building AR/MR applications is showed.

5.3 Hardware

The most common hardware systems for AR/MR are as follows.

5.3.1 Microprocessor Development Boards

The most notable feature of these kind of hardware devices is that they are cheap and easy to program. The two most important are:

– Arduino [10]: an inexpensive open hardware platform, suitable for the creation of interactive physical objects by developers that range from amateur to professional. Designed with the sharing of ideas, knowledge, and collective experiences in mind, it consists of a board with a cheap microprocessor and several I/O ports. It can be obtained either assembling its components by hand or purchasing a ready to use board. Its development software and environment are based, respectively, on Wiring [11] and Processing. It makes easier the use of electronic devices and the development of hardware for AR/MR projects and can be also connected to computer software frameworks such as Flash, Processing, Max/MSP, or Pure Data. IncreTable [12] is an example of an Arduino-based project.

– Gainer [13]: a Gainer board has a microcontroller, USB port, LEDs, sensors, and actuators that the user can access via several PC development environments like Flash, Max/MSP, and Processing. It is very suitable for user interface development and media installations, and it can be acquired in several preassembled configurations, being possible to add new elements or modifying these basic configurations on demand.

5.3.2 Videogame Devices

The use of devices initially designed for video gaming is feasible in AR/MR applications using open and proprietary software development kits (SDKs). Examples of these devices are:

– Nintendo Wii [14]: it is the console that introduced an interaction device able to detect the player's movements, instead of the traditional joysticks or gamepads. Despite the absence of an official SDK, some indie developments appeared on the Internet [15] enabling the use of this device, called Wii remote, as an ideal peripheral to interact with AR/MR applications.
– Microsoft Kinect [16]: it was the answer from Microsoft to the proposal from Nintendo. Firstly developed for the Xbox 360 console, Microsoft offers an official development kit for Windows 7 PCs from June 2011, and a new hardware version for PC is already available. Over this time period several unofficial SDKs appeared, as Open NI [17] or Open Kinect [18]. Microsoft Kinect lets the user interact with the console through a multimodal user interface that recognizes gestures, voice commands, objects, and images, without the need for physical contact related to any traditional videogame controller.
– SONY PS3 Move: after not being commercially successful with its Eyetoy cam for PlayStation 2 console, SONY developed the SONY PS3 Move system, a videogame controller for the PlayStation 3 console, based on movement sensors. It consists of two different components: a main controller and a camera called PlayStation Eye. The main controller has the movement sensors and a sphere that is illuminated. The purpose of the cam is detecting the position of the main controller. It is noteworthy that Sony itself made available an official SDK for this device [19].

5.3.3 Smartphones and Tablets

Modern mobile devices use to have a camera, accelerometer, GPS, large resolution screens, and quite powerful processors. All these features, added to its small size and portability, make them a suitable platform for AR/MR applications. They can be classified by their operating system:

– iOS: when Apple released iPhone, iPad, and iPod touch, development of apps for iOS operating system soon grew exponentially. AR/MR-based apps found a perfect platform on it.
– Android: since Google released its own mobile Operating System, it has been adopted by several manufacturers, and app development for Android rivals that of iOS in volume and quality.
– Symbian: this was the OS proposed by NOKIA, which also supported app development for its smartphones, but it has finally ended in failure, with Nokia announcing in January 2013 that it stops manufacturing Symbian devices [20]. Just mention that there were developers who chose this operating system to run its AR/MR applications.
– Windows Phone: Microsoft, knowing its underdevelopment at this subject and considering NOKIA's disadvantage, tried to give uniformity to the appearance of its popular Windows with a new environment that allows development of "Metro style" apps that eventually will rival to those of iOS and Android.
– Blackberry: with its own operating system installed on its popular smartphones with physical keyboard and its tablet Playbook, it has been another target for AR/MR developers.

5.3.4 PCs and Laptops

Although they have been apparently relegated to a secondary role by mobile devices, popular PCs and laptops (Windows, Mac OS, or Linux) were the first targets of AR/MR developers. An example, based on PCs with a webcam, was [21], developed for the Esquire Magazine: some markers were included on the pages of the magazine which allowed an AR experience by downloading a small SW application and exposing the markers to the webcam.

5.4 Software

After reviewing hardware-related devices and platforms, several software tools allowing developing AR/MR applications over such devices are listed.

5.4.1 Development Frameworks

– ARToolkit [22]: provides a framework to develop real-time AR applications. It uses C/C++ as programming language over several platforms. It also supports languages as Java or Matlab and it is open source. In 2009, FLARtoolkit (ARToolkit+Flash) supposed a revolution in the development of AR applications [23]. There are derived tools such as SLARToolkit [24] which supports Silverlight and Windows Phone.

- Processing [25]: it is open source software providing a development environment to create images, animations, and interaction. It is cross-platform and uses Java as programming language. It allows working with markers and includes libraries to interact with the real world through network connection and with generic hardware devices or even Arduino boards through serial port.
- GART [26]: it was created to easy develop AR applications for Windows Phone. Instead of markers, it is based on the so-called Geo AR: geolocation-based AR which makes use of data taken from the sensors (GPS and accelerometer) and the browsing history of the device.

5.4.2 AR Browsers

- Metaio [27]: a multiplatform tool that offers several solutions for AR/MR development. It includes a plug-in that enables the integration of the developed projects into Junaio [28], a commercial AR browser from the same company.
- Wikitude [29]: it is an AR browser available for iOS, Android, and Blackberry. It also provides an SDK to let developers integrate their own apps with the platform.
- Layar [30]: an AR browser available for the most popular platforms. Similarly to Wikitude, the company provides an associated authoring tool called Layar Creator.
- Mixare: it is an open source AR browser published under GPLv3 license [31], available for iOS and Android.
- BlippAR [32]: an image recognition app, available for iOS and Android, able to show AR animations over a set of patterns, preregistered in an in-app catalogue. This catalogue may be fed by customers of the company, whether brands or individuals.
- Aurasma [33]: an image recognition app, with commercial support for individuals or brands in order to upload their promotional AR contents based on registered image patterns (similarly to BlippAR). It's available for iOS and Android.

5.4.3 Authoring Tools

- DART [34]: multiplatform authoring tool based on Adobe Director. It uses markers for the generated AR applications.
- D'FUSION: AR authoring tool developed by D'FUSION [35].
- BuildAR [36]: multiplatform author tool to develop markers based AR applications.

Table 5.1 AR/MR development tools

SDK/tool	Language	Hardware
BuildAR	–	Mac OS/Windows
Metaio/Junaio	–	Android/iOS/Windows/Web
ARToolkit	C/C++	Android/iOS/Windows Phone/Web
DART	Lingo	Mac OS/Windows
PTAM	C/C++	Mac OS/Linux/Windows
Vuforia	C/C++	Android/iOS
Wikitude	Java/C	Android/iOS/Blackberry
Layar	Java	Android/iOS/Blackberry/Symbian
D'FUSION	C/C++	Android/iOS
AR23D	Java/C	Android/iOS/Blackberry/Symbian
Mixare	Java/C	Android/iOS
GART	C	Windows Phone
Processing/Wiring	Java	Arduino
Gainer	Flash Max/MSP Processing	Gainer
Kinect for Windows SDK	C/C++	Microsoft Kinect
Move.me	C/C++	SONY PS3 Move
BlippAR	–	Android/iOS
IN2AR	–	Android/iOS
STRING AR	–	iOS
AURASMA	–	Android/iOS

5.4.4 Software Libraries

– PTAM [37]: camera tracking system for AR. It's been developed using C/C++, and it can be compiled on several platforms.

5.4.5 SDKs

– Qualcomm's Vuforia: Qualcomm introduced a SDK for development of AR applications called Vuforia [38] with multiplatform support.
– AR23D [39]: this company offers licensing for the SDK (AR 3D SDK) to third party developers.
– IN2AR [40]: a multiplatform tool that lets the developer creating AR content using popular editors like Flash or Unity3D.
– String [41]: only available for iOS, with fully supported integration with Unity3D.

At Table 5.1 software tools reviewed are listed with the corresponding hardware platforms and programming languages to develop AR/MR applications.

5.5 Standards

While all these AR-related tools and technologies emerge and evolve on their own, several standards for AR are emerging; ARML [42], currently reviewed by W3C, is an example. Proposed by Mobilizy, the creators of Wikitude World Browser, it is based on the standard for location-based content called Keyhole Markup Language [43] developed by Google. In addition, the AR Standards Community [44] seeks to collect/monitor progress and activities with a special emphasis on detecting complementary, redundant, or overlapping work and then providing a neutral/grass roots driven environment (platform) to coordinate open and interoperable AR development.

5.6 Applications and Projects

Research and development in Education, Gaming and Entertainment, and Cultural or Industrial knowledge domains has made great use of AR/MR tools and solutions. A list of recent projects is presented in this section.

Education has been one of the main fields of interest, with projects like Avalon [45], which uses an MR environment as a tool for Spanish language teaching. Invizimals [46], from Novorama [47] (for the Sony PSP console) and ARDefender [48] (for the Android and iOS mobile platforms) are examples of videogames that use AR. In the field of industrial applications, Virtualware [49] developed a project for the Spanish Postal Service [50] that visually simulates the size of the shipments. Duran Duran Project [51] is an example of AR application for entertainment and live performance that showed AR images using a system based on projectors and giant markers. Other good example of the same type of application for AR is Augmented Mirror [52] that shows the audience a virtual character, animated in real time by the performance of a hidden human actor. AR projects like ObservAR [53], more suitable for museums, are becoming common in the Culture and Arts field. Other potential scopes for AR/MR research and development can be Healthcare services (Surgery, ER), Military, Architecture, Marketing, or Tourism.

5.7 Conclusion

AR/MR most extended applications are the ones based on mobile devices and the ones related to motion-controlled videogames. This deals with the ease and the small financial investment required to develop and publish applications in the mobile app markets, such as Google Play for Android devices or the Appstore for iPhone/iPad, and the availability of sensors such as GPS and web data that ease the integration of virtual content over digital video. On the other hand, for AR/MR-specific purpose applications, development with Open Hardware platforms is also presented as a good alternative, even for relatively inexperienced electronic developers. In short, there are an increasing number of tools for creating and distributing AR applications which, in conjunction with the widespread use of mobile devices, suggests that AR may end up becoming a commodity in the next years. Industry seems to agree with this statement, with companies like Metaio, which recently unveiled an agreement with ST-Ericsson about its own hardware IP, called AREngine [54], an AR performance accelerating processor for mobile devices.

References

1. Azuma, R. (1997). A survey of AR. *Presence-Teleoperators and Virtual Environments, 6,* 355–385.
2. Milgram, P., & Kishino, F. (1994). A taxonomy of mixed reality visual displays. *IEICE Transactions on Information Systems, E77-D*(12), 1321–1329.
3. Google Glass Project. (2012). A Taxonomy of mixed reality visual displays IEICE Transactions on Information Systems, Vol. E77-D, No. 12. (December 1994) by Paul Milgram, Fumio Kishino. http://g.co/projectglass
4. Haller, M., et al. (2007). *Emerging technologies of AR: Interfaces and design.* Hershey, PA: IGI Global.
5. Lepetit, V. (2008). On computer vision for AR. Computer Vision Laboratory, Ecole Polytechnique Fédérale de Lausanne, Lausanne 08/2008; doi:10.1109/ISUVR.2008.10 ISBN: 978-0-7695-3259-2. In proceeding of: Ubiquitous Virtual Reality, 2008. ISUVR 2008.
6. Henrysson, A., Billinghurst, M., & Ollila, M. (2006). *AR tennis.* Boston: International Conference on Computer Graphics and Interactive Techniques (SIGGRAPH) 2006: Emerging Technologies, 30 Jul–3 Aug 2006. ACM SIGGRAPH 2006 Emerging Technologies, Article No. 1.
7. Reitmayr, G., & Schmalstieg, D. (2002). A platform for location based augmented reality applications. *ÖGAI Journal, 21,* 1.
8. JMonkeyEngine. (2012). http://jmonkeyengine.com/
9. Open Wonderland. (2012). http://openwonderland.org
10. Arduino. (2012). http://www.arduino.cc/es/
11. Wiring. (2012). http://wiring.org.co/
12. Leitner, J., Haller, M., Yun, K., Woo, W., Sugimoto, M., & Inami, M. (2008). IncreTable, a mixed reality tabletop game experience. In Proceedings of the 2008 International Conference on Advances in Computer Entertainment Technology (ACE '08) (pp. 9–16). New York: ACM. doi:10.1145/1501750.1501753; http://doi.acm.org/10.1145/1501750.1501753.
13. Gainer. (2012). http://gainer.cc/
14. NINTENDO Wii. (2012). http://www.nintendo.com/wii
15. Lee, J. C. (2008). Hacking the Nintendo Wii remote. *IEEE Pervasive Computing, 7*(3), 39–45. doi:10.1109/MPRV.2008.53; http://dx.doi.org/10.1109/MPRV.2008.53.
16. Microsoft Kinect. (2012). http://www.microsoft.com/en-us/kinectforwindows/
17. Open NI. (2012). http://wiki.etc.cmu.edu/unity3d/index.php/MicrosoftKinectOpenNI
18. Openkinect. (2012). http://openkinect.org/wiki/MainPage
19. SONY PS3 Move. (2012). http://us.playstation.com/ps3/playstation-move/move-me/
20. Nokia Corporation. (2013). Nokia Corporation Q4 and full year 2012 Interim Report.
21. Esquire. (2012). http://www.esquire.com/the-side/augmented-reality
22. ARToolkit. (2012). http://www.hitl.washington.edu/artoolkit/
23. flash.tarotaro.org. (2012). http://flash.tarotaro.org/blog/

24. SLARToolkit. (2012). http://slartoolkit.codeplex.com/
25. Processing. (2012). http://www.processing.org
26. GART. (2012). http://gart.codeplex.com/
27. Metaio. (2012). http://www.metaio.com/
28. Junaio. (2012). http://www.junaio.com/
29. Wikitude. (2012). http://www.wikitude.com/
30. Layar. (2012). http://www.layar.com/
31. Mixare. (2012). http://www.mixare.org
32. BlippAR. (2013). http://blippar.com/
33. AURASMA. (2013). http://www.aurasma.com/
34. DART. (2012). http://ael.gatech.edu/dart/
35. D'FUSION. (2012). http://www.t-immersion.com/
36. BuildAR. (2012). http://www.buildar.co.nz/
37. PTAM. (2012). http://www.robots.ox.ac.uk/gk/PTAM/
38. RA SDK Qualcomm. (2012). http://www.qualcomm.com/solutions/augmented-reality
39. AR23D. (2012). http://ar23d.com/augmented-reality-sdk.html
40. IN2AR. (2013). http://www.in2ar.com/
41. STRING AR. (2013). http://www.poweredbystring.com/
42. Lechner, M., & Tripp, M. (2010). ARML an augmented reality standard MobileARSummit. Retrieved from http://www.perey.com/MobileARSummit/Mobilizy-ARML.pdf.
43. Keyhole Markup Language. (2013). http://www.opengeospatial.org/standards/kml/
44. AR Standards Community. (2013). http://www.perey.com/ARStandards/
45. Ibáñez, M. B., Kloos, C. D., Leony, D., Rueda, J. J. G., & Maroto, D. (2011). Learning a foreign language in a mixed-reality environment. *IEEE Internet Computing, 15*(6), 44–47.
46. Invizimals. (2012). http://www.invizimals.com
47. Novarama. (2012). http://www.novarama.com/
48. ARdefender. (2012). http://ardefender.com/
49. Virtualware. (2012). http://virtualwaregroup.com/
50. RA CORREOS. (2012). http://virtualwaregroup.com/realidad-aumentada-correos/
51. Saforrudin, N., Zaman, H. B., & Ahmad, A. (2011). Technical skills in developing AR 302 application: Teachers' readiness. *Visual informatics: Sustaining research and innovations.* Lecture Notes in Computer Science Volume 7067, pp. 360–370.
52. Vera, L., Gimeno, J., Coma, I., & Fernández, M. (2011). *Augmented mirror: Interactive augmented reality system based on Kinect.* Human-Computer Interaction – INTERACT 2011. Lecture Notes in Computer Science Volume 6949, pp. 483–486.
53. Gimeno, J., Olanda, R., Martinez, B., & Sanchez, F. M. (2011). *Multiuser augmented reality system for indoor exhibitions.* Human-Computer Interaction – INTERACT 2011. Lecture Notes in Computer Science Volume 6949, pp. 576–579.
54. Metaio AREngine. (2013). http://www.metaio.com/products/arengine/

Chapter 6
A VRPN Server for Haptic Devices Using OpenHaptics 3.0

Maria Cuevas-Rodriguez, Matthieu Poyade, Arcadio Reyes-Lecuona, and Luis Molina-Tanco

Abstract This chapter presents an implementation based on the Virtual Reality Peripheral Network (VRPN 07.30) to handle connectivity between Virtual Reality (VR) applications and SensAble® Technology Phantom Haptic Devices using the OpenHaptics 3.0 Haptic Library Application Programmable Interface (HLAPI). VRPN offers a client–server-based architecture to support network-transparent connectivity between VR applications and a set of physical interaction devices. In this context, VRPN provides a set of classes to handle various physical device types. The proposed implementation consists of (a) new VRPN classes that support connectivity between a haptic device server and VR applications, allow to specify arbitrary 3D object information to haptically render geometries, and report applied force, angle at contact point, Surface Contact Point (SCP), and Depth of Penetration (DOP) and (b) an upgrade of the Phantom dedicated VRPN class to handle haptic rendering using the OpenHaptics HLAPI to manage device state and force computation.

6.1 Introduction

During the last decade, Virtual Reality (VR) applications have included a wide variety of 3D interaction techniques and devices. Among them, the iteration between Virtual Environments (VE) and the user used to be through two senses: the sight and the hearing. Nevertheless, the touch sense is becoming more important and studied

M. Cuevas-Rodriguez (✉)
Departamento de Tecnología Electrónica, Universidad de Málaga, Malaga, Spain
e-mail: mariacuevasrodriguez@gmail.com

M. Poyade • A. Reyes-Lecuona • L. Molina-Tanco
Departamento de Tecnología Electrónica, Universidad de Málaga, Malaga, Spain
e-mail: matthieu.poyade@uma.es; areyes@uma.es; lmtanco@uma.es

V.M.R. Penichet et al. (eds.), *New Trends in Interaction, Virtual Reality and Modeling*,
Human-Computer Interaction Series, DOI 10.1007/978-1-4471-5445-7_6,
© Springer-Verlag London 2013

in VR because it gives the user the possibility of interact and modify the environment. In this context, haptic devices play a really useful role in VR; they are very important as they have allowed a wider multimodality, beyond the traditional visual and auditory stimuli. In addition, haptic devices are bidirectional and allow a more natural interaction closing the perceptual-motor loop between the user and the VE [4]. For these reasons, many applications can benefit from using haptic devices to enhance interaction and providing a realistic force feedback to the user. Specifically, motor skill training applications need haptic interaction in order to be valid.

Haptic rendering is, however, very demanding in terms of computing power. Hence, for many applications a dedicated computer is required in order to provide realistic force feedback. This leads to the problem of connecting the computer or computers where the graphical rendering is being performed and the computer managing the haptic rendering [5]. There is an additional issue with manufacturers of haptic devices providing different programming interfaces. A standard way of efficiently accessing any haptic device through a local network connection would make it easier to use these devices for a wider range of applications.

These issues had to be tackled in the ManuVAR project. The ManuVAR project funded under the European Union's Seventh Framework Programme (NMP-CP-IP-211548) aimed to use virtual and augmented reality to develop an innovative technology platform and a framework to support high value manual work. One of the goals of this project was to provide a flexible platform where different technological elements and methodologies could be connected in a modular way. Therefore, some mechanism was needed for connecting haptic devices with a device-independent and network-transparent interface.

Exactly for these purposes, the Virtual Reality Peripheral Network (VRPN) was developed 10 years ago [7]. VRPN is an open source package, which provides a network architecture for connecting different interaction devices to a VR application. It has become a *de facto* standard for motion capture systems and tracker devices. However it is less popular for other kinds of devices. In its distribution, VRPN implements simple force feedback device classes for SensAble® products, with very limited functionality. For that reason, it is hoped that this work will help in contributing to VRPN becoming also a standard middleware for the integration of haptic devices in VR environments.

This chapter reports a new implementation of a VRPN server which provides the original tracker and button interfaces along with new and varied force device interfaces for SensAble® devices, using the OpenHaptics 3.0 Application Programmable Interface (API) [1], updating and extending the functionalities available in the current VRPN distribution (VRPN 07.30). This new VRPN server can manage the three different models of haptic devices manufactured by SensAble®: the Phantom® Onmi, Phantom® Desktop, and Phantom® Premium 3.0.

The remaining of the chapter is organized as follows: Sect. 6.2 gives a short overview of VRPN and SensAble® Software Developer's Toolkit (SDKs), Sect. 6.3 presents the main features of the proposed implementation, Sect. 6.4 briefly presents an application where it is being tested, and, finally, Sect. 6.5 summarizes giving some conclusions of this work.

6.2   Technical Background

Haptic technology in VR offers a 3D multimodal real-time sensory motor interaction paradigm that feedbacks force sensory information, leading to improve task performance and enhance the way users interact within VEs [4].

SensAble® Technologies is a developer of haptic interfaces that manufacture the Phantom® haptic devices since 1993 [6]. Different models of haptic devices are available as previously mentioned. Each of these devices is shaped as *stylus interactuators* and able to deliver force feedback and high degrees of maneuverability within VEs providing the same feeling experimented by touching a surface with the point of a pencil.

A C++ SDK to support haptic rendering for integration of the haptic interaction paradigm in VEs is provided by SensAble® Technologies. General Haptic Open Software Toolkit (GHOST) is a legacy API for Phantom® devices and currently superseded by the OpenHaptics Toolkit, an Open GL-based library. The OpenHaptics 3.0 toolkit presents a three-layer architecture: the Haptic Device API (HDAPI), the High-Level API (HLAPI), and the micro QuickHaptics API. HLAPI is a high-level API able to haptically render geometries stored into OpenGL's specific buffers. It offers several commands to set custom force effects (stiffness, damping, static and dynamic friction, viscosity, etc.) and handle the thread management required to support haptic rendering. HLAPI manages three different threads: the client thread ($\sim$30 Hz) supports graphical rendering, the collision thread ($\sim$100 Hz) supports collision detection, and the servo thread ($\sim$1,000 Hz) handles the position and orientation of the haptic device and calculates forces.

The combination of a computer graphics engine and a force feedback haptic rendering engine results in a heavy computational load. An option to maintain performance is to execute the graphics and haptics rendering loops in separate computers [5]. VRPN offers a network-transparent architecture to handle connectivity between VR applications and physical interaction devices. VRPN provides a set of classes defining several *canonical interface types*. Each *canonical class* derives into a remote client interface class and a device server interface class. Both specify methods to be called from a remote client and the device server. Devices are mapped into one or several canonical interface types depending on the information reported. Generic interface types consist of Tracker, Button, Analog, Dial, and Force devices. In overall, a purely physical device dedicated class that inherits from one or several interface server types supports the device rendering.

At the time of writing, the currently available version of the standard distribution of VRPN is version 07.30. This version supports connectivity with Phantom® devices through the canonical classes vrpn_Tracker, vrpn_Button, and vrpn_ForceDevice [7]. These provide, respectively, the functionality of a Tracker that reports device position, orientation, velocity, and acceleration; Button that reports device buttons state; and Force Device that handles haptic parameters specifications and reports applied force and Surface Contact Point (SCP).

An additional class, vrpn_Phantom, is responsible of the communication between the haptic devices and the three canonical classes previously mentioned. It is the responsible of the haptic rendering for these specific devices which inherits from the Tracker server, Button server, and Force Device server dedicated classes.

6.3 Implementation

The main goal of this work is to make easier the management of haptic devices through the development of two new classes to be included in the last version of VRPN server. These classes provide innovative and useful functionalities allowing a haptically render of arbitrary geometries.

A new client has been also developed in order to test the described client–server architecture which allows the interaction with the VE. It is also in charge of creating the graphic scene and sending its characteristics to the server to reproduce the haptic scene.

6.3.1 New Classes Implemented

The proposed implementation consists of a new vrpn_ForceDevice class, named *vrpn_ForceDevice_Uma* (Fig. 6.1), and a new vrpn_Phantom class, *vrpn_Phantom_Uma* (Fig. 6.2).

The new vrpn_ForceDevice_Uma class, as the original one, supports connectivity between a haptic device server and VR remote client applications, reporting applied force and SCP. However, this new class allows specifying arbitrary 3D objects information to haptically render geometries and reports not only applied force and SCP but also angle at contact point, Depth of Penetration (DOP), and the identifier of the object that has been touched.

The new vrpn_Phantom_Uma class implements OpenHaptics HLAPI functionalities to manage device states and haptically render force effect models to provide force feedback. These two new classes have been implemented following the philosophy and structure tree of the original classes of VRPN. The vrpn_Phantom_Uma class inherits from the tracker and button canonical classes provided by VRPN and the new force device server class (vrpn_ForceDevice_Uma) as shown in Fig. 6.2.

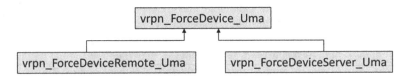

Fig. 6.1 VRPN class hierarchy for Force Device classes

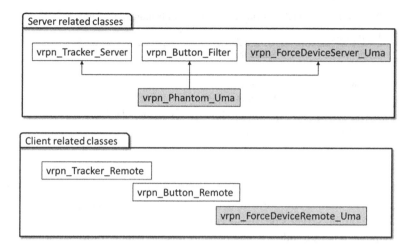

Fig. 6.2 Modifications to the VRPN

Table 6.1 New methods added to vrpn_ForceDeviceRemote_Uma interface

New methods	Description
setObjectNumber	Sets the number of objects to render
setVertex	Sets the vertex of an object
setTransformMatrix	Sets the transformation matrix for each object, which provides orientation, position, and scale of the object
setEffect	Sets the environmental effects to render. HLAPI provides four effects: constant force, spring, viscosity, and friction. For each one, gain, magnitude, frequency, duration, position, and the direction can be provided
startEffect	Indicates that the effect should begin
stopEffect	Indicates that the effect should finish
setHapticProperty	Sets the haptic properties of an object: stiffness, damping, static and dynamic friction, pop through, and mass
setEnvParameters	Sets the force effects which are used to generate ambient sensations: gravity and inertia
setTouchableFace	Sets the face of the object that will be haptically rendering: front, back, or both. This feature is the same for all objects
setWorkspace	Sets the work space, the space where the device is going to interact with the VE

The function of each class is summarized in the following paragraphs.

vrpn_ForceDevice_Uma. This class manages message type declaration and message encoding and decoding. This class increases the functionalities of the original vrpn_ForceDevice class, developing new message types and encoding and decoding functions related to implemented methods described in Tables 6.1 and 6.2 to respectively support connectivity to remote client and device server.

Table 6.2 Send methods within the new vrpn_Phantom_Uma interface

Send methods	Description
sendForce	Sends the applied force
sendDOP	Sends the Depth of Penetration
sendSCP	Sends the Surface Contact Point
sendIsTouching	Indicates if it is touching an object
sendTouchedObject	Sends the identified of the object that this is touching
sendAngle	Sends the angle at contact point

vrpn_ForceDeviceRemote_Uma. This class provides a set of new methods (Table 6.1) for the client application. These methods enable sending haptic parameters, defined in the client application, to be integrated with haptic rendering on the server side. Furthermore, vrpn_ForceDeviceRemote_Uma class implements a set of callback functions to receive haptic information messages from the server.

vrpn_ForceDeviceServer_Uma. It handles a set of callbacks to receive haptic parameter definition messages from the client decoding and forwarding the messages to vrpn_Phantom_Uma class.

vrpn_Phantom_Uma. The new vrpn_Phantom_Uma class has direct communication with the device using the OpenHaptics HLAPI. This class organizes within a set of structures, the received haptic parameters inherited from the vrpn_ForceDeviceServer_Uma class. vrpn_Phantom_Uma performs the haptic rendering providing force feedback to user through the phantom device. Moreover, vrpn_Phantom_Uma class provides force feedback data to the remote client application when any change happens (Fig. 6.3). To do so, a set of methods has been implemented as detailed in Table 6.2.

The only device-specific class is vrpn_Phantom_Uma. To integrate a different force feedback haptic device, a new class has to be implemented with the SDK of the specific device. The rest of the classes are device independent and can be reused, in the spirit of VRPN.

6.3.2 Client–Server Communication

Decoupling graphical and haptic rendering enables parting the asynchronous execution of both systems. On one hand, the client computes the graphical rendering and shows the graphic scene to the user, providing the auditory and visual stimuli. On the other hand, the server carries out the haptically render as it has mentioned in the previous section.

At the beginning of the communication, the client application sets the graphic scene and creates a vrpn connection to the VRPN server, then sets and sends haptic scene properties to force device server (see sequence diagram in Fig. 6.4), firstly by recovering geometry-based information about the objects deployed in the scene from graphics dedicated buffers using the setObjectNumber, setVertex, and

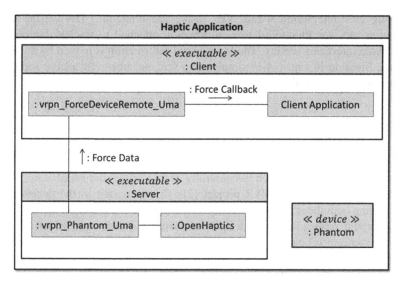

Fig. 6.3 The force feedback changes are sent from the Phantom Device to the Client Application through callback invocation

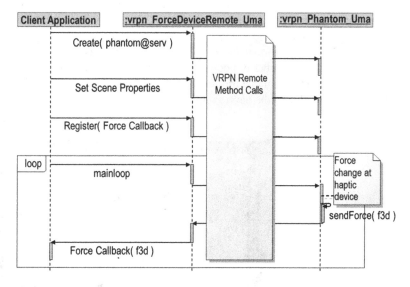

Fig. 6.4 Client–server communication between Client Application and Haptic Device

setTransformMatrix methods detailed in Table 6.1 and, secondly, by defining haptic effects and force model parameters using the methods setEffect, setHapticProperties, setEnvParameters, setTouchableFace, and setWorkspace. The client application starts the force effects and the haptic rendering loop and declares a set of callback functions to enable receiving phantom-based information from the server.

During user interaction within VEs, using the Phantom® Device, the client application receives Phantom-based information attached to tracker, button, and force device interfaces servers. The force-based information is named by the Force Callback function in Fig. 6.4 to simplify the scheme; however, all the supported methods are defined in Table 6.2.

6.4   Application

This implementation has been successfully tested in an industrial case within the framework of the ManuVAR project [2]. This consisted in the development of a training simulator for performing metallographic replicas (Fig. 6.5). The metallographic replica is a non-destructive inspection technique which requires following some specific steps, including a careful polishing of the surface where the replica is going to be taken. The simulator includes a wide variety of scenarios where different objects are rendered. Thanks to the server properties, allowing haptically render of any geometry, the haptic dimension was incorporated into the scene in a quick and easy way.

Within ManuVAR, a distributed platform has been developed to integrate different applications where the connection of any interaction device is location transparent; furthermore, the computational cost of running these applications is allocated in various machines.

The proposed implementation using VRPN has also been successfully used in an experiment where a high number of people tested the simulator to determine which feedback is most appropriate in that training tool. Everybody agreed with the natural and real-world feeling due to the haptic sensation.

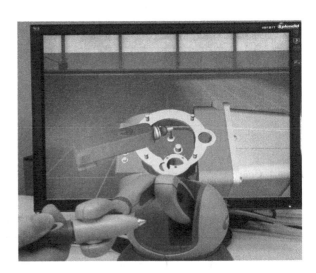

Fig. 6.5 Application case using the Phantom-based VRPN server

An experimental study carried out at the University of Nottingham investigated the design of augmented feedback for improving virtual reality haptic training in the performance of a complex inspection task in a real manufacturing case study [3].

6.5 Conclusion

In this chapter a new VRPN server implementation of force feedback for SensAble® haptic devices is introduced and described. These new contributions include some features, not developed in the current distributions of VRPN. Furthermore, the server provides an easy and efficient way to introduce the haptic dimension in a virtual scene due to the new developed interfaces that offer the possibility of introducing any kind of geometry. Haptic Phantom® device contacts with the virtual geometry and much information about its interaction is reported by the VRPN server.

The work has been developed within the ManuVAR project, where a modular, flexible, and location transparent architecture required a distributed connection of VR devices. All the features described in this chapter have been introduced in that project providing the required results.

These implementations could be the beginning of a new trend of standardizing the haptic device integration in virtual environments using VRPN thanks to the simplicity and modularity of its development.

Acknowledgment The abovementioned research has received funding from the European Commission's Seventh Framework Programme FP7/2007–2013 under grant agreement 211548 "ManuVAR."

References

1. Itkowitz, B., Handley, J., & Zhu, W. (2005). The openHaptics toolkit: A library for adding 3D touch navigation and haptic to graphics applications. In *Proceedings of the Eurohaptics Conference, 2005 and Symposium on Haptic Interfaces for Virtual Environment and Teleoperator Systems* (pp. 590–591).
2. Krassi, B., D'Cruz, M., & Vink, P. (2010). ManuVAR: A framework for improving manual work through virtual an augmented reality. In *Proceedings of the AHFE 3rd International Conference on Applied Human Factors and Ergonomics, AHFE*, Miami, Florida, USA, 17–20 July, 2010.
3. Langley, A., Sharlples, S., D'Cruz, M., Patel, H., Poyade, M., Reyes-Lecuona, A., & Molina-Tanco, L. Impact of multimodal feedback on VR training for manufacturing manual work. In *Proceedings of the Tenth International Conference on Manufacturing Research* (Vol. 1, pp. 219–224). Birmingham, UK, September 2012.
4. Mac Lean, K., & Hayward, V. (2008). Do it yourself haptics: Part ii [tutorial]. *Robotics & Automation Magazine, IEEE, 15*(1), 104–119.

5. Mark, W., Randolph, S., Finch, M., Vanverth, J., Taylor, I., & Russell, M. (1996). Adding force feedback to graph ics systems: Issues and solutions. In *Proceedings of the 23rd Annual Conference on Computer Graphics and Interactive Techniques* (pp. 447–452). ACM, SIGGRAPH 96.
6. Massie, T., & Salisbury, J. (1994). The phantom haptic interface: A device for probing virtual objects. In *Proceedings of the ASME Winter Annual Meeting, Symposium on Haptic Interfaces for Virtual Environment and Teleoperator Systems* (Vol. 55, pp. 295–300). Chicago, IL.
7. Taylor, I., Russell, M., Hudson, T., Seeger, A., Weber, H., Juliano, J., & Helser, A. (2001) VRPN: a device- independent, network-transparent VR peripheral system. In *Proceedings of the ACM Symposium on Virtual Reality Software and Technology* (pp. 55–61). ACM. VRST 01, November 15–17, 2001, Banff, Alberta, Canada.

Chapter 7
Tangible User Interfaces: A New Trend in Interaction for Helping Children with Down Syndrome to Develop Reading Skills

Pedro C. Santana and Bárbara Paola Muro Haro

Abstract This chapter describes the results of a research study implementing a teaching technological strategy to help Down syndrome children develop their reading skills. The study employed the pedagogical method proposed in "Down syndrome: reading and writing" (DSRW) book, augmented with tangible interfaces, resulting favorable results when tested on kids with this syndrome. This study was developed in three stages: First, a direct observation was conducted to help us understand the context of applying the DSRW methodology in sessions with Down children without any technological strategy involved. The second stage included a preliminary evaluation of a first prototype, created to test the reaction of a child with Down syndrome when is exposed to the tangible technology. Finally, the third stage consisted in the evaluation of a second prototype; this prototype was informed on the results of the preliminary evaluation and is more similar to the conceptual design.

7.1 Introduction

In Mexico, one of every 700 births is a child with Down syndrome [1]. By 2010, in Mexico there were 5′739,270 handicapped people of which 8.5 % are mentally disabled and 16.3 % are born with a disability [2]. Thirty years ago, most people with Down syndrome could not read. The reason is that it was considered that they had no ability to do so, and in case of having it, it was thought that it would be useless [3]. Nowadays, there are several methods for teaching reading and writing to children with Down syndrome, for example, "Down syndrome: reading and writing" (DSRW). DSRW is a book that explains a method developed in 1970. It was published in 1991 and it uses a perceptual-discriminative approach to teach these

P.C. Santana (✉) • B.P. Muro Haro
University of Colima, 333 University Avenue, Colima, Mexico
e-mail: psantana@ucol.mx; pao_muro@ucol.mx

V.M.R. Penichet et al. (eds.), *New Trends in Interaction, Virtual Reality and Modeling*,
Human-Computer Interaction Series, DOI 10.1007/978-1-4471-5445-7_7,
© Springer-Verlag London 2013

children to read before they are 5 years old. The priority and fundamental purposes in this method is that the student understands what he reads, fluently, to remain motivated and to keep his interest in reading [4]. One of the conditions of Down syndrome is the deficit of attention. Even though they present this problem, the student will pay attention to the activity if it is of his interest. It is hard for him to concentrate when only oral information is being presented to him, it is therefore appropriate to incorporate other kind of stimulations [5]. In this sense, it was thought of an interesting, stimulating, and fun way to expose these children to this learning methodology. Tangible interfaces have been proved to offer certain benefits in supporting education [6] and had been tested on children with autism (condition that also presents attention deficit) showing favorable results [7]. This chapter will present the positive results produced when adapting the DSRW methodology in an interactive technology using tangible interfaces when tested on kids with Down syndrome.

7.2 Previous Work

Technology supports us in all areas of human life, including education and, recently, special education. Human–Computer Interaction (HCI) is the study of the interaction between humans, computers, and the developed tasks; it is focused mainly in knowing how people and computers can interact to perform tasks through systems and software [8]. Nowadays, HCI is very important in the creation of technologies focused in being used by people, and this importance becomes relevant when working with disabled people. An investigation about existent work that combines technology and HCI, for people with Down syndrome, is presented below.

7.2.1 Methodologies for Teaching Writing and Reading to People with Down Syndrome

7.2.1.1 LATCH-ON

LATCH-ON is a program of the University of Queensland, Australia. It was developed and put into practice in 1998 [9], especially for young adults with Down syndrome who have had education through their lives. It proposes to impulse the habit of reading using several university libraries, museums, and technology (computers). This program lasts 2 years.

7.2.1.2 Down Syndrome: Reading and Writing

A methodology based in the learning pedagogy of perceptual-discriminative learning. The method is presented in a book [10] which explains from the foundations, theory, and data about Down syndrome, its pathology, and ways of learning the correct usage of the method, and it also includes the material for its implementation.

7.2.1.3   See and Learn Language and Reading

This is a program of activities designed for visually strong learners such as Down syndrome children meant to be. It consists of three stages and five steps: Stage 1: Learners are taught 60 common words without going through the reading comprehension process and learn the name–object relation. Stage 2: The learners are taught 16 written words and learn how to join words. Stage 3: Learners are able to assemble simple sentences with the more of 70 words that they already have in their vocabulary, teaching certain key words to join sentences [11].

7.2.2   Technology for the Education of People with Down Syndrome

7.2.2.1   Sound Beginnings 2

This software allows the selection of proper sounds, phonemes, and words; it also allows uploading and use own images [12]. It can-be configured to fit specific requirements.

7.2.2.2   Clicker

It is software designed to teach reading and writing by using images and sounds, creating relations, putting sentences together, etc. [13]. It develops hearing abilities, it encourages practice to speaking skills with "talking books" created by the professor, and it focuses on the form of the language using sentence which is separated in its different components (subject, verb, and complement), in which every component is inside a box of a different color.

7.2.2.3   My First Number Game

This is a touch application developed for iOS devices [14]. It is an application that was not designed for people with Down syndrome, but the Down Syndrome Association of Queensland (DSAQ) has acknowledged it as a useful teaching resource for this condition. It teaches numbers from 1 to 20.

7.2.3 Technology for the Learning of Reading and Writing for Children with Down Syndrome

7.2.3.1 I Like to Read

This is a software [15] developed by the Down Syndrome Association of Granada (GRANADOWN). Its main characteristics are as follows: it uses a global methodology and is individualized, success oriented, and applied in a playful and motivating way and using visual material. The research of the state of the art in the area shows that there are very few technologies applied to the teaching of reading and writing to people with Down syndrome. It is also noticeable that most of the teaching methods are based on the perceptual-discriminative pedagogy, but each one has its own limitations.

7.3 Down Syndrome: Reading and Writing

AS mentioned before, DSRW is a book that explains a method that uses a perceptual-discriminative approach to teach children with Down syndrome to read.

DSRW uses educational material with specific colors, sizes, and fonts that will facilitate the learning process; this material is customizable and adaptable, for it to fit each student's needs and learning level. Prior using this method, it is recommendable that the kid had already participated in a perceptual-discriminative learning program. It is not a problem if the child has not started to talk, but it is a mandatory that he knows that people, animals, things, and actions have names. For example, when the child hears the word "*ball*," he knows what object we refer to, and, even though he does not pronounce it, he locates and evokes it.

The advantages of presenting a graphic written word (which is always accompanied by oral information) to the learner versus oral presentation are two: On the one hand, there is double stimulus because it goes through the visual and auditory pathway; and the written word stays in sight the whole time, which makes it easier to fix it in memory [16].

7.4 Using the Method

An example of the use of the method will be explained.

Material

Image card. It contains an image and underneath the written word that represents it (Fig. 7.1 left side).

Fig. 7.1   Image card and word card

Word card. This card has written on it the same word that is represented in the image card (Fig. 7.1 right side).

Use Example

The adult (teacher or parent) reads the word in the image card repeatedly pointing at it with his finger. Later, he asks the child to read the word in the card. The adult shows the child the word card and points the fact that both cards (image and word cards) have the same word written on them and then asks him to read what the cards say. After that, the adult indicates to the child to put one word on top of the other saying "put *la casa* over *la casa*." The purpose of this exercise is that the learner relates the written words with its correspondent image and the sound of reading it, and, in the future, the learner would be able to recognize the word without the image.

7.5   Tangible Interfaces

Tangible interfaces give physical form to digital information, employing physical objects both as representations and controls for computational media. Tangible user interfaces (TUIs) match physical representations (e.g., spatially easy to use physical objects) with digital representations (e.g., graphics and audio), yielding user interfaces that are computationally mediated but generally not recognizable as "computers" per se [17].

It has been proven that using tangible interfaces offers some benefits in supporting teaching [6]; they have been tested on children with autism, which is a condition with attention deficit that is also found in the DS, demonstrating favorable results [7]. Studies alike [18] show that they are useful because they promote an active participation, which helps with the learning process. These interfaces do not intimidate non-expert users and encourage exploratory, expressive, and experimental activities.

7.6   Understanding the DSRW Method

The followed methodology is based on the User-Centered Design approach, which helped us to understand the context of applying the DSRW methodology in the sessions with children without any technological strategy involved.

The used technique for this case of study was direct observation. Direct observation is when the researcher is placed in personal contact with the fact or phenomenon under investigation.

The observations were performed at the Down Institute of Colima. Three sessions with children of different ages and at different levels of the method were observed and recorded in video for later analysis.

The book of DSRW [10] mentions three stages of the reading learning process:

- First stage: Global perception and recognition of written words
- Second stage: Recognition and learning of syllables
- Third stage: Progress in reading

Our samples were Ricardo, who is in stage 1 of learning; Alex, in stage 3; and Fernando, in stage 2.

After observing these sessions and analyzing the videos, we got the following findings.

7.6.1   Ricardo

The main problem with Ricardo was his lack of attention and interest after a few minutes of work. He is distracted by any sound, loses interest, and starts to yawn. The technique that the teacher uses to get back his attention is to ask him to do some exercises with his hands, like touching his nose, and in other moments, she "threatens" him with sending him to his classroom and ending the session.

7.6.2   Fernando

Fernando yawns a lot from the beginning of the session. He pays more attention to the activities but shows certain resistance to do them. When the teacher asks for his help to do something, Fernando answers that he does not want to help her, so the teacher acts as if the answer hurts her feelings and then Fernando agrees to do the activities. The teacher uses the technique of giving him activities where he has to draw something, because she knows that drawing is an activity that Fernando enjoys a lot.

7.6.3   Alex

With Alex we observed a smoother session, his attention is rarely away from the activities, and it is noticeable that he gives a little more thought to his answers. In contrast with the other two students, he only yawned once in the entire session. Also, when he answers correctly and the teacher congratulates him, he smiles and shows a little more motivation.

After analyzing the observations, the following was concluded. As a professor applying the method, it is important to know your students, to know how to get their attention, and to engage them into the activities. Also, it is necessary to learn not to show negative reactions when the student makes a mistake and to praise him when he does things right. Regarding the students, most of them show a lack of interest in the activities, and it is notable in their lack of attention. This could be because of the deficit of attention presented in their condition or maybe because the sessions took place early in the morning. We notice that it is necessary to motivate learners with interactive activities, because when they are only repeating words (which is an important part of the method), it is when they show the most lack of interest and boredom.

7.7   The System

Using the results previously mentioned as a starting point, tangible interfaces will be used in this investigation [19] with the purpose of proving its feasibility. The design proposed here is a multi-touch interactive concept that integrates tangible elements and software applications maintaining pedagogical precision. The idea for the user interface is a tabletop and a set of digitally augmented tools that would include the educational material used in DSRW (word and image cards), and they will be tagged with augmented reality tags so they can be recognized by the software.

7.7.1   Design and Architecture

As it was mentioned before, our system proposal is the combination of a tabletop with tangible interfaces and software.

The tabletop consists of a table with a clear surface, almost transparent, where the cards of the educational material will be projected, and at the same time, it allows the reading of the augmented reality tags by a web camera. The tangible interfaces will be physical objects representative of the images or words that are presented to the students. These objects have underneath augmented real tags which are read by a web camera placed under the table. The camera sends the reading to the software specially created for our prototype. This prototype processes it and recognizes if the tag of the toy corresponds to the word card or image card projected on the table, and based on this, it provides feedback to the user. The software has the characteristics for allowing the adult to create and customize the cards, save certain cards and the sequence that he designs for a specific session with the kid, and also store data from the sessions, like the number of right and wrong answers. Our system also allows the user to move between the cards and activities with gestures like a flick or a tap.

7.8 Preliminary Evaluation

A first prototype was created to test the reaction of a child with Down syndrome when a tangible technology is presented to him, the way he might interact with it and see if it generates any interest in the child. This prototype was made using a tablet with a touch surface. The tablet was in the middle of a wooden frame to represent the tabletop. Some toys were chosen to be converted into tangible interfaces.

7.8.1 Testing the First Prototype

The potential advantages of tangible interfaces cannot be perceived until they are situated in an interaction context. Preliminary evaluations are an ideal mechanism to go beyond current practices and allow us to get involved in the design process and visualize new schemes of application in a simple and economic way [20]. To explore the feasibility of the conceptual design, a preliminary evaluation was conducted, testing the prototype with a kid with Down syndrome, his parents, and a teacher (see Fig. 7.2). These evaluations were recorded and photographed.

The evaluation took place in the child's house. It included two main phases. First, the parents were informed about the process and the method was discussed. Later,

Fig. 7.2 Preliminary evaluation

we showed the prototype to the student pointing its functionalities and we explained to him the activities to be carried out in the session.

Before initiating the test, we presented to the student the words that were used in the evaluation and performed a few warm up exercises so he would remember the method. Finally, the tasks were applied through a scenario of use.

7.8.2 Preliminary Evaluation Results

After analyzing the videos and the observations of the evaluators, the following was concluded: During the preliminary evaluation, the student with Down syndrome found interesting and exciting the fact that the system improves the interaction that the kid generally has with the method.

During the whole session a constant attention and a permanent expression of joy and interest were noticeable. An important result was that the child maintained his attention in the activities all the time, without the need of instructions or additional encouragement for him to continue working. By the end of the session, the child did not want to stop interacting with the prototype, and he, by his own initiative, continued working with it.

7.9 Improving the Prototype

After the preliminary evaluation, we noticed that in order to have a better context of the interaction with the system and observe the reactions of the learners, we needed to create a prototype informed by the preliminary evaluation results.

The tabletop was built (see Fig. 7.3), the interaction software was created, and we used the same tangible objects of the previous evaluation. In addition, we created physical word cards to be used as tangible interfaces in order to perform a complete cycle of exercises (relation word-image).

7.9.1 Final Evaluation

The test took place in the Down Institute of Colima facilities with three children, the same three who were object of the direct observation conducted at the beginning of this study. For this evaluation, one evaluator, three observers, and the two teachers in charge of the application of the DSRW method in the school attended the sessions.

The sessions were video recorded and the observers took photographs and notes. The evaluation was carried out following a protocol of evaluation that described each step along the whole test, as follows. First, we applied a structured interview

Fig. 7.3 The tabletop
prototype

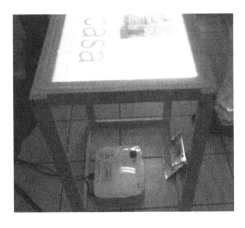

to the teacher asking her experience in special education and, more specifically, with the method. Then, we explained to her the concept of the system, the design, and the functionality of the prototype. Finally, we asked some questions about the opinion that the teacher could create about the system from the given explanation. After the introduction with the teacher, the evaluation started. The sessions with the students took no more than 20 min. All the sessions started with the evaluation team introducing themselves and giving a brief introduction of the reasons of why the student was there and what was wanted from him.

Following the introduction, the evaluation started with a warm up exercise as a reminder of the method where the student read four image cards projected on the tabletop. The words used in all the educational material for this evaluation were the house (*la casa*), the car (*el carro*), the bed (*la cama*), and the chair (*la silla*).

After the warm up exercise, each student performed three activities:

- Reading of four word cards projected on the tabletop
- Relation of the tangibles with the projected word cards on the tabletop
- Relation of the tangibles with the projected image cards on the tabletop

At the end of the three evaluations with the learners (see Fig. 7.4), a final interview was made to the teacher asking her observations in the sessions about the reaction of the children, differences between the activities carried out in a traditional way and the ones using the system, and also their general opinions.

7.9.2 Results

Thanks to the analysis of the videos, the notes and the observations from the evaluator, the observers, and the teachers, the following results were obtained.

During the sessions, the students showed interest and curiosity when interacting with the prototype. They were anxious to handle the tangible interfaces and place

Fig. 7.4 Final evaluation

them where they were asked to. One of the students, a shy one, made the "thumb up" signal to his teacher when he thought the evaluator was not watching.

The opinions of the teachers were very positive, mentioning "*I observed that they (the learners) were fascinated*" and said that maybe the learners would learn faster with the interaction that the system allows them to have and that having this kind of technology would make them feel more integrated to society because then they would also know how to use technology.

One of the teachers made a comparison with software that the kids use in computers at school called "activities with Pipo," saying that with the computer, the learners need to interact with the mouse and it is not very easy for them, and if they do not have a monitor, they get bored because of this. With the prototype, the fact that the material is tangible and easily manageable, it complements the activities and makes the interaction much easier.

The general opinion of the first teacher was "wow!" and she would really like to use the system once it is finished. The second teacher commented that she was very interested in learning how to implement the system in regular classes.

7.10 Conclusion

This work proposes to improve the process of the learning of reading of children with Down syndrome through the usage of tangible interfaces. An interactive system was designed that presented favorable results in a preliminary evaluation, taking into account that the measures were the interest of the user with Down syndrome towards the system and the focused attention to the activities.

In the final evaluation, the results were very pleasant, because it was used a more faithful prototype to the concept design, also measuring the acceptance of the users with Down syndrome. The users showed enthusiasm, curiosity, excitement, and desire to participate in the activities. In addition to this, the system obtained good reviews from the teachers that attended the evaluation sessions. They also showed enthusiasm towards the system, wanting to learn how to use it and asking for it to be presented to the institution once it is finished.

With the implementation of this system we pretend to generate a positive impact on the kids with Down syndrome and, eventually, support the DSRW method to perform better through the use of technology.

Our further work consists of the enhancement of the prototype to have even closer to the desired final design and test it in long terms. In this third evaluation we want to measure the progress through several months and comparing it to the teaching of the method in a traditional way. The final objective is to see if the learning process with our system is faster and better than the traditional one.

Acknowledgments We thank the Down Institute of Colima for their collaboration and facilitations for us to do our study and tests. Thanks to the IHCLab Research Group at the University of Colima for their help in the realization of the tests and building the second prototype.

References

1. Cruz Martínez, Á. (2008). México, rezagado en socialización de personas con síndrome de Down. *La Jornada*. 25 de Abril de 2008.
2. INEGI. (2010). Discapacidad en México. http://cuentame.inegi.org.mx
3. Down 21. (200). Lectura y escritura. http://www.down21.org/web_n/index.php?option=com_content&view=article&id=1136:lectura-y-escritura&catid=92:educacion&Itemid=2084
4. Troncoso, M. V. (2000). Características de los alumnos con síndrome de Down. http://www.down21.org/web_n/index.php?option=com_content&view=article&id=1136%3Alectura-y-escritura&catid=92%3Aeducacion&Itemid=2084&limitstart=3
5. Troncoso, M. V., & Del Cerro, M. (2001). Características del método. http://www.down21.org/web_n/index.php?option=com_content&view=article&id=1136%3Alectura-y-escritura&catid=92%3Aeducacion&Itemid=2084&limitstart=3
6. Marshall, P. (2007). Do tangible interfaces enhance learning?. In *Proceedings of the 1st international conference on Tangible and embedded interaction (TEI '07)* (pp. 163–170). New York: ACM.
7. Keay-Bright, W. (2008). Tangible technologies as interactive play spaces for children with learning difficulties: The reactive colours project. *The International Journal of Technology, Knowledge and Society, 4*(1), 111–120.
8. Martínez de la Teja, G. M. (2007). Ergonomía e interfaces de Interacción Humano-Computadora. In *IX Congreso Internacional de la Ergonomía* (p. 8). México.
9. Moni, K. B., & Jobling, A. (2000) LATCH-ON: A program to develop literacy in young adults with Down syndrome. *Academic Research Library, 44*, 40–49.
10. Troncoso, M. V., & Del Cerro, M. M. (2009). Síndrome de Down: Lectura y escritura. *Fundación Iberoamericana Down 21.*
11. International Down syndrome Education. (2011). See and Learn. http://www.seeandlearn.org/en/gb/language-reading/
12. Black, B. (2006). Educational software for children with Down syndrome -an update. *Down Syndrome News and Update 6*(2), 66–68.
13. Crick Software Ltd. (2011). Clicker & Special Needs – Speech or Language Impairments. Obtenido de Clicker & Special Needs – Speech or Language Impairments. http://www.cricksoft.com/us/products/tools/clicker/special-needs/speech/speech.aspx

14. Inc., Down Syndrome Association of Qld. (2011). Technology for children and adults with Down syndrome. http://dsaq.probitypartners.com.au/down-syndrome-information/technology
15. Álvarez Martínez, S., & López-Moratalla López, I. (2008). *Me gusta leer: método de lectura global con soporte informático*. Granada: Proyecto Sur Industrias Gráficas, S.L.
16. Troncoso, M. V., & Díaz-Caneja, P. (2000). Perspectiva histórica. http://www.down21.org/web_n/index.php?option=com_content&view=article&id=1136%3Alectura-y-escritura&catid=92%3Aeducacion&Itemid=2084&limitstart=2
17. Ullmer, B., & Ishii, H. (2000). Emerging frameworks for tangible user interfaces. *IBM Systems Journal, 39*, 3–4.
18. Carreras, A., & Parés, N. (2007). Diseño de una instalación interactiva destinada a enseñar conceptos abstractos. Interacción'07. Zaragoza, Spain.
19. Santana Mancilla, P. C., & Muro Haro, B. P. (2011). Tangible interfaces to support the teaching of reading and writing to children with down syndrome. *IEEE Learning Technology Newsletter, 13*(2), 9–12.
20. Santana, P. C., Castro, L. A., Preciado, A., González, V. M., Rodríguez, M. D., & Favela, J. (2005). Preliminary evaluation of Ubicomp in real working scenarios. In: *The Proceedings of the 2nd Workshop on Multi-User and Ubiquitous User Interfaces (MU3I) at IUI 2005*. San Diego, California, USA.

Chapter 8
Designing a Communication Platform for Ubiquitous Systems: The Case Study of a Mobile Forensic Workspace

Carlos Rodríguez-Domínguez, Kawtar Benghazi, José Luis Garrido, and Aurora Valenzuela Garach

Abstract The ubiquitous computing is a human-computer interaction model in which information systems (i.e., ubiquitous, pervasive or ambient intelligence systems) are seamlessly integrated into the lifestyle of the user. In particular, these systems offer information about the user context and cooperate with other systems to facilitate some everyday tasks. As a consequence, interoperability is a key requirement for them, since it is usually necessary to exchange information between heterogeneous platforms (operating systems, middleware solutions, hardware architectures, etc.). Interoperability requirements are usually fulfilled by establishing shared communication protocols (SOAP, JSON, IIOP, and so on) and connection mechanisms (for instance, Wi-Fi or BlueTooth). Therefore, the software trends to be highly bond to specific communication-related technologies, making it increasingly complex to incorporate future communication technologies that could enhance its quality. In this paper we present several platform independent models to overcome this problem by decreasing the level of cohesion between communication technologies and software for ubiquitous computing. As a case study, and to show their applicability, the models have been implemented through specific technologies to support the development of a mobile forensic workspace.

C. Rodríguez-Domínguez (✉) • K. Benghazi • J. Luis Garrido
ETSIIT, Department of Computer Languages and Systems, University of Granada,
Granada, Spain
e-mail: carlosrodriguez@ugr.es;benghazi@ugr.es;jgarrido@ugr.es

A. Valenzuela Garach
Faculty of Medicine, Department of Forensic Medicine, Toxicology and Physical Anthropology,
University of Granada, Granada, Spain
e-mail: agarach@ugr.es

V.M.R. Penichet et al. (eds.), *New Trends in Interaction, Virtual Reality and Modeling*,
Human-Computer Interaction Series, DOI 10.1007/978-1-4471-5445-7_8,
© Springer-Verlag London 2013
97

8.1 Introduction

Current computing environments are increasingly adopting the ideas of the ubiquitous computing interaction model [29], mainly due to the success of mobile devices, like smartphones and tablets. As a consequence, the fulfillment of the technical and quality requirements associated to ubiquitous computing environments has begun to be the focus of many research and development works.

One key research field is to find new communication models to allow the interoperability between the entities of a ubiquitous system (services, applications, agents or devices) through the exchange of information while positively affecting the overall quality of the system (efficiency, scalability, reusability, maintainability, etc.). In contrast with traditional computing systems, in ubiquitous systems, entities exchange information in a shifting networking environment [4] where heterogeneous communication technologies usually have to coexist [7] (middleware solutions, networking technologies, communication protocols, and so forth). Moreover, interoperability involves establishing shared communication protocols (SOAP, IIOP, and so on) and connection mechanisms (for instance, Wi-Fi or Bluetooth) [27]. For example, in home automation environments, users usually remotely interact with their home devices from their mobile phones through a combination of specific protocols, like KNX [13] or LonWorks [6], with more general purpose ones, like SOAP [9] or IIOP [24].

In this way, since communication protocols and specifications are very quickly outdated due to the increasing demands of the consumers (speed, range, power consumption, etc.), software developers, in many cases, have to re-implement existing software in order to accommodate new communication technologies or, in other cases, they have to incorporate these new technologies by combining them with the previously existing ones, in an effort to maintain backward compatibility [1]. However, in both cases, software solutions are highly bond to specific communication technologies [22], which decreases maintainability [28] and increases production costs each time software is updated [18].

In this paper, the objective is to overcome some of the previous issues by decreasing the level of cohesion between communication technologies and software entities in ubiquitous systems. The main idea is to separate software from specific communication technologies by using technology-independent models that assist in the design of the communication aspects of these systems. The models also promote an easier software development and integration of different protocols and mechanisms, thus enhancing software interoperability, while not decreasing its maintainability.

The remainder of the paper is structured as follows: In Sect. 8.2 some background knowledge related to the proposal presented herein is described. Section 8.3 introduces the models to support the communication functionalities associated to ubiquitous systems. Section 8.4 presents a case study that stems from an implementation of the proposed models intended to support a shared and ubiquitous workspace for forensic experts. In Sect. 8.5, we discuss the benefits and drawbacks of the proposal. Finally, Sect. 8.6 summarizes conclusions and possible lines of future work.

8.2 Foundations on Communication Platforms
for Ubiquitous Systems

Ubiquitous systems should meet some specific requirements, like mobility support, that traditional communication technologies, like CORBA [23], do not currently accomplish [15]. Consequently, specialized solutions are often required. For example, some of the most remarkable middleware technologies for ubiquitous systems [10] are:

- *STEAM* [17]: PubSub-based middleware. It is able to manage groups of nearby users. It also provides partial support for power management, mobility, and interoperability between heterogeneous platforms.
- *EMMA* [20]: Message-oriented middleware. Messages are full preformatted documents. Both one-to-one and one-to-many communications are supported.
- *Expeerience* [3]: Peer-to-peer information exchanging. It supports mobile code and to dynamically discover shared resources.
- *SELMA* [8]: It ensures a balanced resource management between producers and consumers. It supports both mobile agents and the dynamic discovery of nearby entities.
- *Mobile-Gaia* [26]: PubSub-based middleware with coordination support. It provides a WYNIWYG ("what you need is what you get") platform. It supports the management of clusters of entities.
- *LIME* [19]: It implements a tuple-based coordination model.
- *MeshMdl* [12]: Object-oriented tuple space. It supports mobile agents. Makes use of an asynchronous communication model that is known as "Xector."
- *XMIDDLE* [16]: Shared information structured in XML. It is able to manage network disconnections, which are usual in ubiquitous systems.
- *Mate* [14]: Software has to be developed in a specific interpreted programming language. It provides a synchronous communication model and mobility support.

Previous middleware technologies deal with communications in ubiquitous systems in a different manner (i.e., different communication paradigms, protocols, underlying technologies, etc.), focusing on some requirements but not taking into account others. Moreover, in recent years, standard textual protocols, usually based on XML, have overtaken the use of middleware solutions. While their use increases maintainability, and they are easier to understand and use, their efficiency is lower in comparison with the previously mentioned middleware technologies. As a consequence, software engineers have to integrate heterogeneous communication technologies to achieve their goals. For instance, DDS ("Data Distribution Service") is oftenly used to support real-time event distribution, and UPnP or Apache River (Jini) is a software framework to support dynamic discovery of nearby entities. This composition of different technologies usually results on the decrease of maintainability and reusability of the developed software [28].

8.3 Models Supporting Communications in Ubiquitous Systems

The extra difficulty of incorporating multiple communication technologies into a ubiquitous system should be balanced with a better availability of powerful techniques providing the needed abstractions to manage development complexity. In this section we propose several technology-independent models related to the basic communication functionalities that should be present in ubiquitous systems [15]:

- *Message exchanging*, that is, one-to-one communications between context aware applications and services
- *Distribution of events* to notify state changes in an application to other applications
- *Dynamic discovery* of nearby entities to exchange messages or notify events

These functionalities allow entities in a ubiquitous system, independently of their nature (a service, an application, a device, etc.) and the used development technologies (protocols, mechanisms, middleware solutions, etc.), to exchange messages (for chats, videoconference, etc.), notify events (UI replication, push messages, etc.), and dynamically discover nearby entities (spontaneous social networks, location-aware ad systems, etc.). The following subsections detail the specific models to support those communication functionalities in a technology-independent manner.

8.3.1 Message Exchanging

Message exchanging is commonly used for one-to-one communications between applications and services. The wide range of requirements associated with ubiquitous systems usually involves integrating several existing technologies and protocols, which usually involves higher development complexity. The technology-independent model depicted in Fig. 8.1 is intended to overcome this drawback. The elements represented in this model are described in Table 8.1.

Message and *Marshallable* elements can be instantiated with different communication protocols to exchange information between heterogeneous *Proxies* and *Servants* through one or more *CommunicationChannels*. These technology-independent concepts enable the integration of different technologies, thus enhancing software interoperability while promoting the separation between the operational logic and the specific underlying technologies. Moreover, *proxies* and *servant* can be considered high-level abstractions over the entities in a ubiquitous system that communicate through message passing.

At functional level, *proxies* communicate with *servants* through *messages* in order to make requests and to receive their corresponding replies. Messages will consist of a set of *marshallables*, that is, a set of values that are codified as specified in a concrete communication protocol. Additionally, the reception of asynchronous

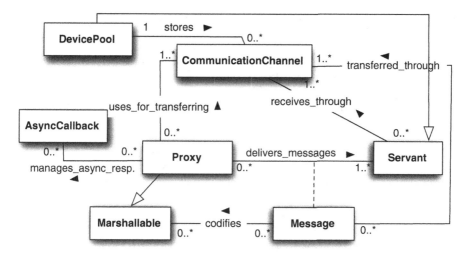

Fig. 8.1 Model to support message exchanging

Table 8.1 A description of the elements in the message exchanging model

Element	Description
Message	Information exchanged between a sender and a receiver (usually between applications and services)
Channel	Abstract specification of a communication technology (middleware solution, protocol, etc.)
Servant	Model of a remotely accessible object
Proxy	Model of a binding to a servant, to "transparently" access remote objects
Marshallable	Model of a codifiable object that can be transferred as part of a message
Async. Callback	Action to be executed whenever an asynchronous message is received
Device Pool	Stores instantiated *communication channels* and provides one in case others are not available

replies is made through *asynchronous callbacks*. The messages are transferred through *communication channels*, which are stored in a *DevicePool*. This pool integrates the needed communication technologies (protocols, middleware solutions, etc.) as instances of a *CommunicationChannel*. Moreover, it could automatically provide one at run time, in case others were not available, so as to provide mobility support. Furthermore, each provided instance of a *CommunicationChannel* could incorporate several mechanisms to support both "off-line" and "online" operation modes within. The goal of these mechanisms could be to transparently store messages that were not delivered and to send them when it becomes possible. It is important to note that the *DevicePool* could be remotely accessible by every entity of an ubiquitous system. This way, all the entities could retrieve shared *CommunicationChannel* instances in order to interoperate with other entities.

Finally, entities may incorporate new instances of *CommunicationChannels* into the system, so as to dynamically support new communication mechanisms.

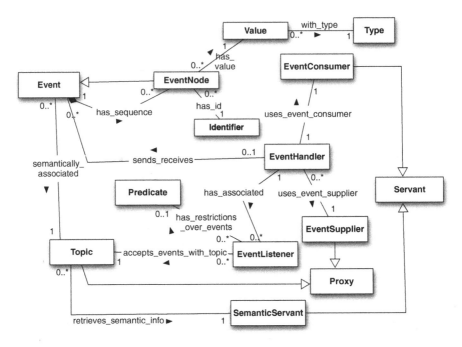

Fig. 8.2 Proposed model to support event notification

For example, if an entity (a) detects that a *CommunicationChannel* instance is not present in the DevicePool, it can store it. From that moment on, another entity (b) could use this new *CommunicationChannel* instance to interoperate with (a). Software developers may use different communication technologies stored in the pool for exchanging information between different proxies and servants, which enhances mobility and interoperability support. For example, some proxies may communicate with servants through WAN connections, while others could make use of PAN connections, depending on their specific requirements (mobility support, efficiency, etc.) and their context (a network infrastructure is unavailable, the device battery has a low charge level, etc.).

8.3.2 Event Notification

Entities may notify events about changes in their internal state to a set of other interested entities. For example, in an instance of a mobile shared workspace, if a shared file is changed, then an event should notify other instances of the same workspace of this occurrence in order to achieve a consistent file state. In Fig. 8.2, the devised event notification model, based on PubSub paradigm, is depicted using a UML class diagram.

Previous model aims to support event notification independently of the technology that is used to implement it. For example, this model could be instantiated using CORBA Notification Service or DDS. Technology independence is mainly achieved by instantiating *EventConsumer* and *EventProducer* elements. Also, although previous figure is simplified, it is possible to access the *DevicePool*, like in the message exchanging model (see Fig. 8.1) in order to retrieve or store specific communication mechanisms that can be shared between the entities of a ubiquitous system, thus contributing to their interoperability.

Events are modeled as a collection of *event nodes*, each of them associated with an identifier and a typed value. Events are associated with semantic information (*topics*) (like in DDS specification), which is stored in a *Semantic Servant*. This way, it is allowed to access shared topics associated with each received event and "topic"-based subscriptions that are enabled.

The elements that provide support for publishing and subscribing to event topics are *EventListeners* and the *EventHandler*. An *EventListener* allows establishing the actions to be executed whenever a notified event is related to a specific topic and accomplishes a specific *Predicate*. *Predicates* enable "content"-based subscriptions. The *EventHandler* is responsible for receiving published events (through a *CommunicationChannel*) and delivering them to the appropriate listeners. The proposed *Event* model is detailed in [25].

At operational level, this event notification model can be used by instantiating *EventListeners* and publishing events through the *EventHandler*. Whenever an event is published, the event listeners should execute their related actions if their associated predicates are fulfilled by the received event. Furthermore, the *EventHandler* and the *EventListeners* could provide high-level abstractions that hide the technologies and mechanisms that are used to publish and receive notifications in ubiquitous systems.

8.3.3 Dynamic Discovery

In ubiquitous systems, entities should be able to dynamically discover other entities that are physically placed around them (or that are accessible through the underlying communication mechanisms) in order to interoperate with them. *How* entities are discovered specifically depends on the underlying technology (i.e., Wi-Fi, Bluetooth, etc.). In Fig. 8.3 it is depicted the proposed model to support dynamic discovery of entities using different underlying technologies. This model consists of a *Mobile Discoverer* that notifies events anytime an entity modifies its reachability status and a *MobileDiscoveryListener*, which receives those notifications and asynchronously executes different actions.

In this case, we have considered that the actions should be always asynchronously triggered, since it is not possible to limit the time needed for executing most of the existing discovery algorithms and the discoverer entity should never stop its execution flow.

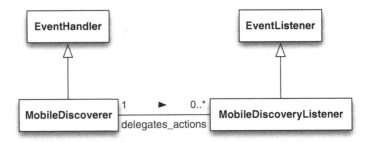

Fig. 8.3 Proposed model to discover nearby entities in a ubiquitous system

8.4 Case Study: A Mobile Forensic Workspace

8.4.1 General Description

Governments and specific police forces (like Interpol) apply protocols of action intended to support victim identification in different scenarios: natural disasters, accidents, terrorist attacks, murders, etc. These protocols try to deal with how victim data is collected and how professionals (e.g., members of police forces and forensic experts) have to cooperate. Currently, governments and police forces do not use supporting technologies for both in situ data collection and cooperation, since it was necessary to fulfill several requirements that, until recently, could not be technologically addressed. In particular, some of the most challenging ones were:

- *Data collection.* Since there are several official protocols intended to support victim identification, it was not possible to specify a uniform data model for collecting and sharing information. Thus, software solutions had to be "customized" for each specific protocol and scenario.
- *Data sharing.* In order to share information in a group or even between different groups (e.g., police and forensic experts), software applications made use of common network infrastructures, like the Internet, which may not be available in some scenarios (e.g., maritime accidents, natural disasters, rural environments).

The mobile forensic workspace intends to assist forensic experts in collecting in situ data about victims while overcoming previous issues. In the workspace it is required to exchange information with nearby applications, devices, etc. so as to support data sharing between forensic experts.

The models presented in previous section have been applied to the design of MFW. The three technology-independent models have been gathered into a middleware, that is, a communication layer intended to separate low-level software/hardware resources from software at application level [2] (in this case, collaborative tools to assist forensic experts while they collect and share data). Figure 8.4 outlines the layers of the logical architecture of MFW.

Fig. 8.4 Overview of the software architecture of the proposal

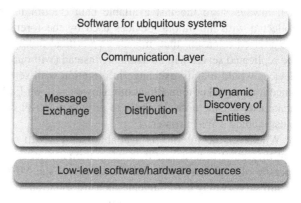

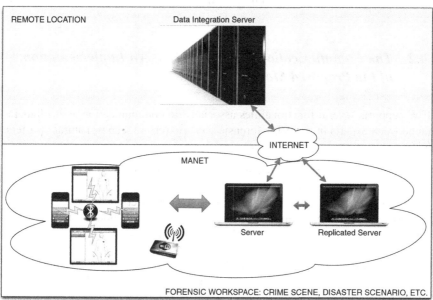

Fig. 8.5 Deployment architecture for mobile forensic workspace

MFW makes use of the deployment architecture that is shown in Fig. 8.5. It is important to remark that, although this architecture is the advised one, none of its elements is totally required, except for the devices to execute the application by final users. This way, professionals, will not be limited, in any case, by the availability of a specific underlying communication technology.

In this architecture, devices can exchange information, for instance, by making use of Bluetooth technology. This way, a network infrastructure is not necessary. These devices exchange information with two servers that could ideally be available in location (as the only basic desirable infrastructure provided by the official institutions that are acting in the disaster, accident, crime, etc.). These servers will always store the last available data (victim information, multimedia, etc.) collected with the mobile devices used by the forensic experts. The two servers are advised to ensure that, in case of a critical failing happens in the main server, the replicated server will be available instead (without losing any data). The mobile devices would mainly exchange information with servers by making use of Wi-Fi since it is a quicker than Bluetooth. However, if Wi-Fi is not available, devices will make use of Bluetooth. In order to provide a Wi-Fi connection, the infrastructure must include a Wi-Fi router.

Whenever the Internet is available, servers will communicate the information that they store to a remote data integration server, which will be dependent of the specific official institution that makes use of the MFW. Additionally, if required, in situ servers may communicate their information to more than one remote server (e.g., more than one official institution, replicated servers).

8.4.2   The Communication Layer in MFW: An Implementation of the Proposed Models

MFW supports several functionalities associated to communication and collaboration between experts in a specific forensic scenario (crime scenes, natural disasters, multiple-victim accidents, and so on):

- *Informal communication.* Support for making voice calls and text messaging between forensic experts.
- *Document authoring.* Collected information about victims is associated to an author and to a time stamp. Documents (texts, images, videos, etc.) and their authoring information are available for every expert in a specific forensic scenario.
- *Concurrent document modification.* Forensic experts are allowed to modify the same document at the same time and to observe other changes in real time.
- *Automatically synchronized changes.* Each change to a document is automatically (and transparently) synchronized between forensic experts, even if they lose their connection and they reconnect after a while.
- *Security and privacy of shared information.* Rules are established for specifying access control, how and which data is exchanged, etc.

These functionalities do not rely on specific communication technologies or mechanisms, since the MFW aims to be adaptable to the requirements of any official authority. On the contrary, the workspace has been designed on top of a specific implementation of the communication models proposed in Sect. 8.3. The implementation of the models is part of the communication layer in MFW. As a consequence, the MFW can be adapted to the needs of any official authority by re-implementing the models in the communication layer, but not the other components in the rest of the software layers.

Table 8.2 Description of the implementation of the proposed interoperability models

Model	Implementation
Message exchange	
Message	Messages are codified using either ICE protocol [30] or JSON [5]. Messages are used to exchange one-to-one information between users (text, images, audio, video, etc.) and to interact with remote services
Channel	An implementation for the Wi-Fi standard and another one for the Bluetooth standard
Event notification	
Event and topic	Events are notified whenever a user changes a document (text, images, videos, etc.), when a user wants to deliver a text message to more than one receiver, or when a user wants to initiate a voice call with another user
Event producer and consumer	If Wi-Fi communications are used, then it is used a centralized service that delivers each event to the appropriate receivers. If Bluetooth is used, then events are delivered through broadcasts
Dynamic discovery	
Mobile discoverer	Two mobile discoverer have been implemented: one for Wi-Fi and another one for Bluetooth communication mechanisms
Mobile discovery listener	A mobile discovery listener has been implemented to show a list of nearby experts to the user. Another one has been implemented to execute an algorithm to synchronize the information stored in the mobile device whenever a new nearby expert is detected

The current implementation of the models for the MFW is described in Table 8.2. The elements that are not described in this table are independent of the communication technology due to their specific design in the proposed models. The implementation is part of an open-source middleware called BlueRose [21].

The MFW has been developed for iOS devices (iPhone, iPad, and iPod touch). Several screenshots of the resulting mobile application are shown in Fig. 8.6.

In previous figure, several functionalities of the MFW are depicted: (a) shared information about a victim, (b) the author of a data entry, (c) a shared whiteboard for drawing an outline of a body description (tattoos, body marks, etc.) over several body pictures (front, back, top, both sides, hands, etc.), and (d) a text and voice chat.

8.5 Discussion

This research work presents platform-independent models related to three communication functionalities that are usually required in ubiquitous systems: message exchanging, event notification, and dynamic discovery of nearby entities. The aim is to decrease the level of development complexity that entails the integration of heterogeneous communication technologies. The models can be implemented for a specific computing platform on the basis of existing communication technologies. They can be also incorporated into a middleware layer that separates low-level

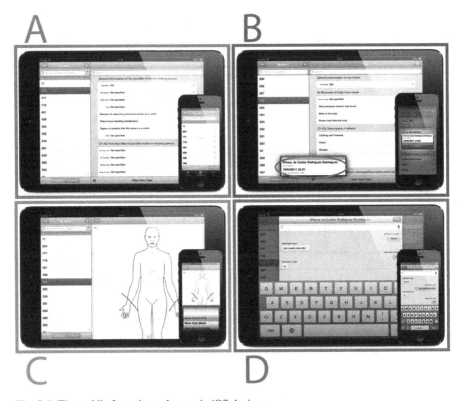

Fig. 8.6 The mobile forensic workspace in iOS devices

software/hardware resources and software at application level. In any case, the implementation of the proposed models is highly reusable, since they are also independent of the end-user software that is built on top of them. The benefit is that the maintainability of the software is improved, since the usage of specific technologies is isolated from the actual implementation of the software solutions, making it easier to detect or mitigate development deficiencies and to meet new requirements in the future.

For instance, in the proposed models, we have tried to separate the implementation of the communication functionalities from the actions that should be executed in the high-level software. As an example, for the discovery of nearby entities, there is a separation between the implementation of the specific discovery algorithm (in the *MobileDiscoverer*) and the actions to be executed whenever an entity changes its reachability in a specific context (in the *MobileDiscoveryListener*). This separation further improves maintainability (for instance, the discovery algorithm should not be related to the specific discovery-related actions to be executed) and reusability (e.g., the actions are usually independent of a specific communication technology and could be reused for different discovery algorithms).

In spite of the benefits of the proposal, it is important to note that, since the models add an extra abstraction level over existing communication technologies, the efficiency of the software that is developed on top of it might be negatively affected in comparison to ad hoc developments. Nevertheless, so far we do not have empirical results nor measures, but current tests and the carried out implementations do not present any observable penalty in efficiency.

8.6   Conclusions and Future Work

The proposal presented herein consists of a set of technology-independent models to support a manageable interoperability between entities (applications, services, etc.) in ubiquitous systems. The models can be incorporated into a middleware layer that separates low-level software/hardware resources and software at application level. A workspace to support collaboration and communication between forensic experts has been presented in order to show the feasibility of the proposal.

As for future work, we aim to incorporate QoS parameters and coordination support to the proposed models. Moreover, an efficiency study should be carried out in order to compare the performance of a system incorporating the proposed models with a system whose communication technologies are incorporated *as is*. Furthermore, the models proposed herein are mainly related to the structural view of the communication functionalities more commonly associated with ubiquitous systems, although a brief description of the behavior is also given. To this respect, we are currently researching development guidelines to help software engineers into incorporating these models into their developments through the mentioned software framework. Also, we are in the process of specifying a high-level model that can better conceptualize the entities in a ubiquitous system on the basis of the models presented. Finally, the communication layer developed for MFW is currently being incorporated to a software framework intended to facilitate the development of context-aware applications and services in ubiquitous systems.

Acknowledgements This research work is funded by the Project P10-TIC-6600 granted by the Andalusian Regional Government and the Project 20F2/36 granted by CEI-BioTIC Granada. This work has also been partially supported by the "Contrato-Programa, Facultad de Educación y Humanidades de Ceuta 2010–2012" of the University of Granada.

References

1. Barton, J. (2004). Software upgrade in ubiquitous computing. In *Proceedings of pervasive*. Vienna, Austria.
2. Bernstein, P. A. (1996). Middleware: A model for distributed system services. *Communications of the ACM, 39*(2), 86–98.

3. Bisignano, M., Calvagna, A., Modica, G. D., & Tomarchio, A. (2003). Expeerience: A jxta middleware for mobile ad hoc networks. In *Proceedings of the 3rd international conference on P2P computing*. Linköping, Sweden.

4. Corradi, A., Lodolo, E., Monti, S., & Pasini, S. (2009). Dynamic reconfiguration of middleware for ubiquitous computing. In *Proceedings of the 3rd international workshop on adaptive and dependable mobile ubiquitous systems* (pp. 7–12).

5. Crockford, D (2006). JavaScript Object Notation (JSON). Tech. rep., RFC 4627, The Internet Engineering Task Force (IETF): Network Working Group.

6. Echelon Corporation: LonWorks. Available online at: http://www.echelon.com/technology/lonworks/

7. Flores, C., Grace, P., & Blair, G. S. (2011). Sedim: A middleware framework for interoperable service discovery in heterogeneous networks. *ACM Transactions on Autonomous Adaptative Systems, 6*(1), 1–8.

8. Görgen, D., Frey, H., Lehnert, J. K., & Sturm, P. (2003). Selma: A middleware platform for selforganizing distributed applications in mobile multihop ad-hoc networks. In: *Western simulation multiconference*. San Diego, CA.

9. Gudgin, M., Hadley, M., Mendelsohn, N., Moreau, J. J., Nielsen, H. F., Karmarkar, A., & Lafon, Y. (2007). *Soap version 1.2 part 1: Messaging framework* (2nd ed.). W3C Recommendation 27. http://www.w3.org/TR/soap12-part1/

10. Hadim, S., Al-Jaroodi, J., & Mohamed, N. (2006). Trends in middleware for mobile ad hoc networks. *Journal of Communications, 1*(4), 11–21.

11. Henning, M. ZeroC ICE 3.4.2 Manual. Available online at: http://www.zeroc.com/Ice-Manual.pdf. Last Accessed Aug 2013.

12. Herrmann, K., Mühl, G., & Jaeger, A. (2007). Meshmdl event spaces – A coordination middleware for self-organizing applications in ad hoc networks. *Pervasive and Mobile Computing, 3*(4), 467–487.

13. International Organization for Standardization (ISO) (2006) Information technology – Home Electronic Systems (HES) Architecture. International Standard ISO/IEC 14543:2006.

14. Levis, P., & Culler, D. (2002). Mate: A tiny virtual machine for sensor networks. In: *Proceedings of the international conference on architectural support of programming languages and operating systems*. San Jose, CA.

15. Maia, M., Rocha, L., & Andrade, R. (2009). Requirements and challenges for building service-oriented pervasive middleware. In: *Proceedings of the 2009 international conference on pervasive services*. London.

16. Mascolo, C., Capra, L., Zachariadis, S., & Emmerich, W. (2002). Xmiddle: A data-sharing middleware for mobile computing. *Wireless Personal Computing, 21*(1), 77–103.

17. Meier, R., Cahill, V (2002). Steam: Event-based middleware for wireless ad-hoc networks. In R. Wagner (Ed.) *Proceedings of the 22nd IEEE International Conference on Distributed Computing Systems Workshops* (pp. 639–644). Vienna: IEEE Computer Society Press.

18. Mukherjee, S., Aarts, E., Roovers, R., Widdershoven, F., & Ouwerkerk, M. (2006). *Amiware: Hardware technology drivers of ambient intelligence*. New York: Springer.

19. Murphy, A., Picco, G., & Roman, G. C. (2006). Lime: A coordination model and middleware supporting mobility of hosts and agents. *Transactions on Software Engineering and Methodology (TOSEM), 15*(3). Retrieved from http://portal.acm.org/citation.cfm?id=1151695.1151698.

20. Musolesi, M., Mascolo, C., Hailes, S. (2005). Emma: Epidemic messaging middleware for ad-hoc networks. *Personal and Ubiquitous Computing, 10*(1), 28–36.

21. MYDASS Research Group: Bluerose. Available online at http://code.google.com/p/thebluerose.

22. Nadiminti, K., Assuncao, M. D. D., & Buyya, R. (2006). Distributed systems and recent innovations: Challenges and benefits. *InfoNet Magazine, 16*(3), 1–5.

23. OMG: Common object request broker architecture (corba) specification version 3.1. part 1: Corba interfaces. OMG specification (pp. 1–540) (2008).

24. OMG: Common object request broker architecture (corba) specification version 3.1. part 2: Corba interoperability. OMG Specification (pp. 1–260) (2008).

25. Rodríguez-Domínguez, C., Benghazi, K., Noguera, M., Bermúdez-Edo, M., & Garrido, J. L. (2010). Dynamic ontology-based redefinition of events intended to support the communication of complex information in ubiquitous computing. *Journal of Network Protocols and Algorithms, 2*(3), 85–99.
26. Shankar, C., Al-Muhtadi, J., Campbell, R., & Mickunas, M. D. (2005). Mobile gaia: A middleware for ad hoc pervasive computing. In *IEEE consumer communications and networking conference (CCNC 2005)*.
27. Strang, T., & Linnhoff-Popien, C. (2003). Service interoperability on context level in ubiquitous computing environments. In *Proceedings of the international conference on advances in infrastructure for electronic business, education, science, medicine, and mobile technologies on the internet (SSGRR2003w)*.
28. Tapia, D. I., Alonso, R. S., De la Prieta, F., Zato, C., Rodríguez, S., Corchado, E., Bajo, J., & Corchado, J. M. (2010). SYLPH: An ambient intelligence based platform for integrating heterogeneous wireless sensor networks. *IEEE International Conference on Fuzzy Systems*.
29. Weiser, M. (1991). The computer for the 21st century. *Scientific American, 265*(3), 94–104. http://doi.acm.org/10.1145/329124.329126
30. ZeroC.: Ice 3.4.2 manual. Available online at: http://www.zeroc.com/Ice-Manual.pdf (2013).

Chapter 9
Gamification: Analysis and Application

Andrés Francisco-Aparicio, Francisco Luis Gutiérrez-Vela, José Luis Isla-Montes, and José Luis González Sanchez

Abstract In this chapter, we present a method for applying gamification as a tool to improve the participation and motivation of people in performing different tasks. We analyse what are the psychological and social motivations of human beings and what game mechanics can help to satisfy these needs. In the same way, we propose a method for analysing the effectiveness of gamification based on a quality service model and the metrics associated with the properties of the playability as a measure of fun induced by the process of gamification.

9.1 Introduction

Since the early 1980s, researchers in the field of Human-Computer Interaction have tried to apply game design elements in contexts that have nothing directly to do with entertainment. Early studies focused on the use of game mechanics that would allow converting user interfaces in more pleasurable interaction systems [1, 2]. Other research emphasised the importance of carrying out further analysis of the meaning of fun [3] and its relation to the concept of usability [4], in order to improve the process of analysis of satisfaction of interactive systems.

In 2010, within the conference that took place at the DICE Summit held in Las Vegas (Nevada), the game designer Jesse Schell gave a talk in which he presented a hypothetical future where video games would be part of our lives [5]. Daily tasks would be related to some kind of game that we would get points and rewards based on our behaviour.

A. Francisco-Aparicio (✉) • F.L. Gutiérrez-Vela • J.L. González Sanchez
GEDES Research Group, ETS de Ingeniería Informática, University of Granada, Granada, Spain
e-mail: andres@ugr.es; fgutierr@ugr.es; joseluisgs@ugr.es

J.L. Isla-Montes
Department of Computer Languages and Systems, Universidad de Cádiz, Cádiz, Spain
e-mail: joseluis.isla@uca.es

V.M.R. Penichet et al. (eds.), *New Trends in Interaction, Virtual Reality and Modeling*,
Human-Computer Interaction Series, DOI 10.1007/978-1-4471-5445-7_9,
© Springer-Verlag London 2013

This fusion of the real and the virtual world through game mechanics is what Jesse Schell referred to gamification. From that moment, the term gamification was acquiring greater relevance and several articles from different fields were published, such as research related to marketing [6, 7] or Human-Computer Interaction [8].

Gamification is defined as the use of game design elements in non-gaming contexts [9]. The elements used in the processes of gamification are related to games, that is, they belong to structured activities with explicit rules and not to spontaneous activities or improvised behaviours. Unlike serious games, that are complete games designed for a primary purpose other than pure entertainment, gamification only uses game elements without constituting a full game itself. The application of the game elements is not limited to digital media nor is linked to any particular technology or any particular design practice [9]. Gamification can be used as a tool to improve the participation and motivation of people in carrying out diverse tasks and activities that generally could not be very attractive. Its application is not restricted to any specific area and can be used in contexts as diverse as education [10], the development of respectful behaviour towards the natural environment [11, 12] or to improve the well-being of the elderly [13].

Currently, the relentless advance of ubiquitous computing driven by the integration of mobile devices in the society has become a particularly interesting scenario for the inclusion of game mechanics in different contexts with the intention of motivating people to perform certain tasks.

In this article we propose a method that facilitates the analysis of tasks that you want to gamify. Based on the macro self-determination theory of human motivation, we define a framework that allows us, on the one hand, to determine what type of game mechanics should incorporate these activities to meet the psychological and social needs of human motivation [14] and, on the other, to assess the effectiveness of the process of gamification based on fun, the properties that characterise the playability and the degree of improvement in obtaining satisfactory results using a quality service model.

9.2 Video Games and Human Motivation

A video game is a computer programme specially created to entertain, based on the interaction between a person and a machine where the video game is executed [4]. Fun and highly interaction are some of the most interesting features of these systems. Thanks to these and other characteristics, video games can be used as a motivational tool of human behaviour [15, 16].

The self-determination theory, proposed by Ryan and Deci, is a macro theory of human motivation concerning people's inherent growth tendencies and their innate psychological needs [14]. According to this theory, intrinsic motivation is the core that is associated with sports and gambling. Intrinsically motivated activities are those that the individual finds interesting and performs without any kind of conditioning, just by the mere pleasure of carrying them out.

To maintain the intrinsic motivation in individuals, it is necessary to satisfy the following psychological and social needs:

- *Autonomy*: Autonomy refers to the sense of will when performing a task. When activities are performed by personal interest, perceived autonomy is high. Providing opportunities to choose, using positive feedback and not controlling the instructions given to people, have been shown to improve the autonomy and, consequently, the intrinsic motivation of individuals [17].
- *Competence*: Competence is the need of the people to participate in challenges and feel competent and efficient. The factors that improve the experience of competition, such as the opportunities for acquiring new knowledge or skills, be optimally challenged [18] or receive positive feedback, improve the perceived level of competition, and therefore it also improves intrinsic motivation.
- *Relatedness*: Relatedness is experienced when a person feels connected to others. Intrinsic motivation will be strengthened in relations that convey security, making this type of motivation appears more frequently and in a more robust way [14, 19]. The current integration between games and social networks is very interesting to use it as a reinforcing motivation.

In one of his books [20], Daniel H. Pink identifies three key elements that allow achieving personal well-being and personal satisfaction: autonomy, mastery and purpose. Autonomy responds to the desire of all people to control their own lives and how they do their jobs. Mastery concerns the desire to constantly improve and achieving personal satisfaction through challenges that fit the capabilities of each individual. The purpose acts as a connecting thread of the intrinsic needs of people and it enables personal fulfilment.

9.3 Description of the Method

From a functional point of view, the game can be split in three in three parts: game core, game engine and game interface. The game core defines the elements that will characterise and differentiate the nature of the game. The game engine handles the representation of each element of the game and how the user interacts with them through a series of software routines, modules or subsystems. The game interface is responsible for displaying the final appearance of the game and for managing the interaction that makes the user with the game, and it presents all content with which the player can interact with, such as options, virtual world scenes or controls [4].

When we want to perform a process of gamification, we will focus mainly on the game core, which defines the game mechanics, the storyline and the user experience. The game mechanics determine the operations and laws that shape the virtual world that is recreated in the video game, the storyline manages the argument of the video game and its narration, and the user experience defines the elements that are related to user interaction [4].

Fig. 9.1 Activities of the
method that we propose

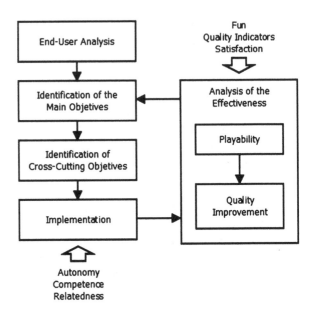

In gamification processes, it is necessary to identify which set of mechanics are most interesting based on the objectives of the task that you want to gamify.

In general, our method can be defined by a basic sequence of activities. The first one is to analyse the types of users who will use the system. The second is to identify the main objective of the task that you want to gamify. In the third activity, we identify one or more underlying objectives that are interesting for people. In the fourth activity, we make a selection of game mechanics in accordance with the context in which the process of gamification is applied. At the same time, we determine the types of interactive experiences that support the selected game mechanics. Finally, in the fifth activity, we analyse the effectiveness of the implementation of gamification based on fun, quality indicators and customer satisfaction and service quality. This last activity is linked to the cross-cutting objectives to define an iterative process.

This sequence of activities proposed can be repeated for each of the objectives or tasks that define the business model you wish to perform the process of gamification.

To make an effective process of gamification, we propose the following activities (Fig. 9.1):

1. *End-user analysis*: Determine who will use the gamified system, what are their motivations, needs, interests and preferences.
2. *Identification of the main objectives*: Identify the main purpose of the task you want to gamify. The main objectives correspond with the main objectives of the business process or any of the objectives of the tasks that are performed in that process. These tasks are normally not motivating and it is desirable to improve its efficiency.

3. *Identification of cross-cutting objectives*: Identify one or more transversal objectives that are interesting to the person. Based on these objectives we will use game mechanics to create a process that improves the interest of the individual and promotes the development of intrinsic motivation.

4. *Implementation*: Selection of game mechanics that match the objectives and support the needs of human motivation (autonomy, competence and relation) and implementation of the gamification process. This process may consist in the creation of a new system or improving an existing one, the development of an advertising campaign, the design of a website and so on. Some examples of these mechanics are:

   - *Autonomy*: The game mechanics that reinforce the autonomy are those that allow carrying out elections and not forcing the user to perform certain actions. It is important to avoid any kind of reward that deflects the internal motivation of the person towards external causality. In the same way, we must avoid the supervision and control of the user's actions since otherwise the feeling of autonomy would diminish. Examples of such mechanisms are profiles, avatars, macros, configurable interface, alternative activities, privacy control and notification control.
   - *Competence*: The perception of competence may be favoured by those mechanics that enable the user to feel competent in the system. In this sense, positive feedback plays a very important role, but it is essential that it does not overlap the perception of autonomy, since otherwise the user will not feel responsible for the actions that have allowed him to achieve this positive situation. In the same way, it is important to adjust the objectives of the activities to the possibilities of each user, providing them with optimal challenges that favour the perception of competence. We must avoid transmitting the user any negative information, since this will impact negatively on his intrinsic motivation. Examples of such mechanisms are positive feedback, optimal challenge, progressive information, intuitive controls, points, levels and leader boards.
   - *Relatedness*: Relatedness is another psychological needs associated with intrinsic motivation. We need to facilitate the mechanics that give support to communication with others and reinforce the relationship between individuals. Also, we must incorporate game mechanics that allow users to both express their ideas as influencing other people. Examples of such mechanisms are groups, messages, blogs, connection to social networks and chat.

5. *Analysis of the effectiveness*: The analysis of the effectiveness of the gamification process must be done from two different points of view. Firstly, we must assess whether the application of gamification generates fun tasks through integration with the game mechanics that have been defined in the system. This aspect is very important, since it constitutes the basis of motivation that is intended to achieve with gamification. In our proposal, this assessment will be based on the analysis of the metrics associated with the property of playability, defined by González [4]. Each of these metrics focuses on a concrete vision of the game and allows

you to measure the player's experience during the process of interaction with the system. On the other hand, these metrics focus on the evaluation of the playability based on the culmination of objectives, something that is in accordance with the method of analysis and application of the gamification that we have proposed.

The analysis of the fun based on the metrics associated with the playability will take place through user testing and through the completion of questionnaires and test users with specific metrics or performing a heuristic evaluation by experts. Secondly, it is necessary to examine whether the process of gamification has generated an improvement in results that meet the objectives of the activities (increase in productive tasks, increase in the number of clients, increase in customer loyalty . . .). To analyse the effectiveness, we use a service quality model and we set quality parameters that match the objectives that we have identified before (activities 2 and 3). Then, we make a comparison between the values obtained prior to gamification process and the results that have been achieved before. This allows us to identify whether the process has been effective and whether the application of game mechanics have resulted in an improvement of the motivation of people, reflected in the completion of objectives.

– *Analysis of fun*: One of the concepts that we must take into account in assessing the effectiveness of the gamification is fun. Video games can motivate people because of the fun they generate. The gamification is at a much more granular level than the video games, but in the same way, it is necessary that the process that is generated after applying gamification is fun for the user. The game mechanics associated with human motivations represent only the structure on which to settle the fun. The confluence of the game mechanics and fun is required to make an effective gamification process.

   The analysis of the playability, which is defined as the set of properties that describe the player's experience in a particular game system, can help us in determining the degree of fun that has a system in which a process of gamification has been conducted. The interaction experiences can be characterised on the basis of a series of attributes present in the usability concept. These concepts acquire different nuances in the video games, complemented with other attributes which together seek to characterise the experience of the player.

   For this analysis, we will adapt the metrics associated with the playability.

– *Selection of quality indicator*: Quality indicator will allow us to assess the effectiveness with which the gamification has been applied to a particular process. In general, any activity can be quantified in a parameter to evaluate the degree of satisfaction achieved and the overall quality that has been reached at the end of the process. The selection of the quality indicator will be linked to the definition of the objective of the task as well as the context in which we are applying gamification. There are contexts in which the indicator can be easily identified, as it could be the case of a support system for teaching in which each person has a qualification related to their academic performance. Quality indicator must be analysed prior to the gamification process in such a way that it can be made a later comparison with data obtained once the game mechanics have been applied.

– *Satisfaction and quality of service*: From the point of view of the services marketing, gamification may be defined as a form of packaging of services in which a basic service is improved using a set of services based on rules that give the user feedback and interaction mechanisms [21]. This definition provides an interesting insight when considering that the gamified service is not which provides mechanisms for interaction and feedback to the user, but one that improves their service thanks to these mechanisms. Moreover, this definition does not take into account the nature of the basic service, which means that a video game could be gamified for creating what we call a meta-game.

In this way, we could analyse quality improvement that has occurred after applying gamification to a service based on a service quality model. From this model, we can determine whether, as a direct cause of intrinsic motivation, there has been an increase in the scope of objectives and whether the overall quality of service has increased.

A service quality model that can be particularly interesting to analyse the gamification is that proposed by Professor Richard L. Oliver of Vanderbilt University [22], later modified by Richard A. Spreng and Robert D. Mackoy [23]. This model seeks to integrate customer satisfaction and quality of service, defining the entities that affect their value.

The quality of service would be determined by comparison of the ideas that has the person regarding the service and performance that has obtained by using it, while satisfaction would be defined based on the comparison of expectations and ideas that had the customer service and expectations and ideas that have not been met. The expectations of the customer would also have influence on performance that is perceived when using the service.

The measurement of the degree of satisfaction and quality of service will be done through questionnaires to each of the entities that are defined in the model. The questionnaires related to the expectations and ideas should be made prior to the use of the service by the customer [23]. The rest of entities will be evaluated using the same method once the client has finished using the service. Finally, we will apply a model of factor analysis to obtain results regarding the entities and their correlations.

This process should be done both before and after applying gamification, to allow comparison of the results and determine if service satisfaction and quality have been increased thanks to the gamification.

The intended purpose of the analysis process is fed back to the activities of cross-target identification and selection of game mechanics. That way we can optimally adjust the transversal objectives to the objectives of the tasks that we are applying the gamification.

9.3.1 Gamification and the Importance of the Analysis of the Playability

In our method, we use the definition of playability as a mechanism to analyse the fun and effectiveness that occurs in a gamification process. The analysis of fun is one of the most difficult and important aspects of the method, so it is important to understand its definition and the concepts on which it is based.

Many authors consider playability as a representative element for the quality of interaction and user fun. Rollings presents the 'triad of playability' [24], which contains three key elements for identifying the fun of an interactive environment: rules of interactions, objectives and goals to achieve.

Ben Shneiderman in 'Designing for Fun: How Can We Design User Interfaces to Be More Fun?' shows that user interfaces for playing should use clear and direct metaphors for the users, applying attractive graphics, animation and sounds, and these types of interfaces improve the fun and the effectiveness of the interaction system [25].

Furthermore, Akihiro Saito [26] indicates that the player experience and fun is identified by 'Gamenics': the quality of play, the quality of the platform on which a programme runs and the mechanics of the interaction (GAme + MEchanics + electroNICS). The work established four principles to consider within the proposed guidelines:

- Intuitive User Interface (emphasising ease of use).
- Interact without manual (the users should not feel confused about what to do and how to do it).
- Interfaces that help overcome the traditional learning curve (producing excitement in the users helped by the device).
- Reality: We should bear in mind that the user is familiar with their environment and context of life, and thus, when designing a programme, we need to provide the user with familiar interaction mechanisms to ensure his or her integration with the system.

Norman [27] and Lazzaro [28] propose that one of the secrets of fun is the management of emotions, where motivation is a key factor in generating a positive experience for the users. If users are continually motivated, the user experience will improve. Lepper and Malone proposed a number of factors that help improve user motivation, namely, challenges, curiosity, control and fantasy [29]. Affective improves the final experience, thanks to the quality of the art facet [30]. Aesthetic of the elements of the system also have influence in the interaction experience evaluation and testing [31].

Playability is based on Usability, but, in the context of fun and video games, it goes much further. Furthermore, Playability is not limited to the degree of 'fun' or 'entertainment' experienced when playing a game. Although these are primary objectives, they are concepts so diffuse as to require definition using a broad set of attributes and properties to measure the Player Experience.

The attributes to characterise the experience of an interactive software are [32]:

- *Satisfaction*: The degree of gratification or pleasure of the player for completing a video game or some aspect of it like mechanism, graphics, user interface, story, etc.
- *Learnability*: The facility to understand and dominate the game system and mechanics (objectives, rules, how to interact with the video game, etc.).
- *Effectiveness*: The necessary time and resources to offer fun and entertainment to players while they achieve the different game objectives and reach the final goal.
- *Immersion*: The capacity to believe in the video game contents and integrate the player in the virtual game world.
- *Motivation*: The characteristics that provoke the player to realise concrete actions and persist in them until their culmination.
- *Emotion*: The involuntary impulse originated in response to the stimulus of the video game and induces feelings or unleashes automatic reactions and conducts.
- *Socialisation*: The degree of the set of game attributes elements and resources that promote the social factor of the game experience in group.

9.4 Application Example

In this example, we will apply the proposed method to a bug tracking system. Bug tracking systems are software applications that allow you to keep a record of any errors that are detected in a software system, as well as information related to the correction of failures.

In the gamification process, we should use game mechanics that are integrated in a natural way in the context of the system, taking into account its objectives and the innate social and psychological needs of the users.

9.4.1 End-User Analysis

The end-users of the system will be those involved in the development of the computer system: developers, analysts, quality software engineers, etc. They are people who use technology on a daily basis and have advanced knowledge of use of different types of software for different platforms.

9.4.2 Identification of the Main Objective

(a) Improve the quality of the bug reports that generate the people who work in the area of software quality assurance. The increase in the quality of error reports makes it possible that the developers can reproduce the error more easily and locate the source of the fault in less time. This speeds up the process of software debugging and reduces the error resolution time.

(b) Improve both the average number of bugs reported weekly and the average error resolution, strengthening the teamwork for the detection, documentation and error correction.

(c) Ensure the quality of the software.

9.4.3   Identification of the Cross-Cutting Objectives

Developers will be interested in resolving errors that have assigned (feeling of success) in the shortest time possible (self-improvement) and with minimal effort, something that we can achieve if we encourage to the developers to solve problems and involve quality workers to improve the error reporting.

9.4.4   Implementation

To implement the gamified system, we will modify the bug tracking system incorporating the set of game mechanics that give support to the objectives that have been identified. Some of the game mechanics that we can apply are:

• Autonomy:

- *Profiles.* The user indicates the area in which he works and his knowledge, the software he uses regularly, the programming languages he knows, as well as personal information.
- *Task selection.* The user can view the list of errors that have been reported and select those that best fit his professional profile and in which he is interested in working.
- *Configurable interface.* The user customise the design of the bug tracking system by modifying the CSS template and adds a custom module to forward to his email the changes that occur in the error that he is working, as, for example, changes in the priority of the bug, change of the department that works on the error, comments from other users, etc.
- *Privacy control.* The user sets as private his date of birth and his phone number in the profile.
- *Notification control.* The user disables notifications of errors that have a low or very low priority.

• Competence:

- *Karma.* The user detects an error and reports it in the bug tracking system. His karma increases by 15 points for reporting a new bug, 5 for attaching screen shots and 10 for completing all fields of the bug reporting form.

- *Positive feedback.* The user reports a new error and the system displays a personalised message of thanks based on the severity of the error, the details provided in the report and the user's karma.
- *Badges.* The user resolves a bug in less time than the average error resolution time and unlocks the 'Fast Hunter' badge.
- *Real-time information.* The system displays the real-time activity of users and also shows links to the new system events, such as adding a new bug report to the system, assigning a bug to a user, a user comments on a bug report, etc.
- *Challenges.* A user challenges another to solve two errors with equal priority in the shortest possible time, betting a certain amount of karma. A working group challenges another group to resolve different errors with same priority.
- *Leader boards.* The system can display different leader boards, for example, depending on the number of bugs fixed, number of errors reported, average time of resolution, average weekly resolution of errors, average weekly reporting of errors, etc.

- Relatedness:

  - *Working groups.* The users create working groups to resolve errors together or to investigate specific parts of the software looking for errors.
  - *Messages.* The system allows sending personal messages between users.
  - *Blogs.* The user creates a new entry in his blog, which recommended a series of effective exercises for the lower body workout.
  - *Connection with social networks.* The user shares on Facebook the achievement and badges that he has achieved and the progression of his karma.

9.4.5   Analysis of the Effectiveness

To analyse the effectiveness that has had the gamification in the company, we must determine, first, whether the application that has been developed is fun for the user and, secondly, if we have managed to increase the level of motivation in workers through the game mechanics. In the same way, we should check if the application of the process of gamification has resulted in an improvement of service and customer satisfaction.

9.4.5.1   Analysis of Fun

To analyse the fun we will do a heuristic evaluation using the metrics associated with the properties of the playability and through the realisation of tests of users that we will distribute among the members of the company.

9.4.5.2 Selection of Quality Indicator

Just as in the identification of the cross-cutting objectives, the selection of the quality indicator is closely related to the objectives of the person. In our case, if the person aims to correct more errors than the rest of his teammates, we may take as a quality indicator the weekly average of error resolution. Tracking the average error resolution will allow us to assess whether there has been an increase in quality after the process of gamification.

9.4.5.3 Satisfaction and Service Quality

To determine the degree of satisfaction and quality of service, we will distribute questionnaires that analyse the wishes, ideas and expectations of the customer before and after the process of gamification. These tests will be distributed among the members of the company and subsequently applies a model analysis of factorial with the intention of collecting the desired information.

9.5 Conclusions and Future Work

In this chapter, we have presented a method of analysis and application of the gamification based on self-determination theory. We have proposed a method consisting of several activities that describe a procedure of analysis and selection of objectives, identification of context, selection of game mechanics and analysis of the effectiveness of the processes of gamification.

We have shown how it is possible to intrinsically motivate people through game mechanics that favour the perception of autonomy, competence and relatedness. In the same way, we have determined the characteristics to be met by game mechanics to motivate individuals. We highlighted that intrinsic motivation requires free partition people in interesting activities that provide optimal and novel challenges.

On the other hand, we have proposed to address the analysis of the effectiveness of the gamification from two different points of view. The first is from the point of view of the fun and using the metrics associated with the properties of the playability. The second is from the point of view of improving the effectiveness of the services, using quality indicators and a service quality model.

Finally, we have shown an example of application of the method in the creation of a gamified bug tracking system, showing examples of game mechanics that may be favourable to increase the intrinsic motivation of workers.

We are currently working on the development of methods of heuristic evaluation for the analysis of the effectiveness of gamification, we are adapting the playability analysis metrics to gamification and we are testing the application of the method in real cases.

Acknowledgments This work is financed by the Ministry of Science and Innovation, Spain, as part of VIDECO Project (TIN2011-26928).

References

1. Malone, T. W. (1980). *What makes things fun to learn?: A study of intrinsically motivating computer games*. Palo Alto: Xerox, Palo Alto Research Center.
2. Malone, T. W. (1984). Heuristics for designing enjoyable user interfaces: lessons from computer games. In *Human factors in computer systems* (pp. 1–12). Norwood: Ablex.
3. Carroll, J. M., & Thomas, J. C. (1988). Fun. *SIGCHI Bulletin, 19*(3), 21–24.
4. González Sánchez, J. L. (2010, July). Jugabilidad: Caracterización De La Experiencia Del Jugador En Videojuegos. Ph.D. Thesis, Universidad de Granada.
5. Schell, J. (2010). Dice 2010: Design Outside the Box, 2010. Conference available at: http://www.g4tv.com/videos/44277/dice-2010-design-outside-the-box-presentation
6. Zichermann, G. (2011). *Gamification by design: Implementing game mechanics in web and mobile apps*. Sebastopol: O'Reilly Media.
7. Zichermann, G., & Linder, J. (2010). *Game-based marketing: Inspire customer loyalty through rewards, challenges, and contests*. Hoboken: Wiley.
8. Deterding, S., Sicart, M., Nacke, L., O'Hara, K., & Dixon, D. (2011, May). Gamification: Using Game-design elements in non-gaming contexts. In *Proceedings of the CHI 2011 Workshop Gamification: Using Game Design Elements in Non-Game Contexts*. ACM.
9. Deterding, S., Khaled, R., Nacke, L. E., & Dixon, D. (2011, May). Gami-fication: Toward a definition. In *Proceedings of the CHI 2011 Workshop Gamification: Using Game Design Elements in Non-Game Contexts*. ACM.
10. Lee, J. J., & Hammer, J. (2011). Gamification in education: What, how, why bother? *Academic Exchange Quarterly, 15*(2), 146.
11. Brewer, R. S., Lee, G. E., Xu, Y., Desiato, C., Katchuck, M., & Johnson, P. M. (2011, May). Lights Off. Game On. The Kukui Cup: A dorm energy competition. In *Proceedings of the CHI 2011 Workshop Gamification: Using Game Design Elements in Non-Game Contexts*. ACM.
12. Inbar, O., Tractinsky, N., Tsimhoni, O., & Seder, T. (2011, May). Driving the scoreboard: motivating eco-driving through in-car gaming. In *Proceedings of the CHI 2011 Workshop Gamification: Using Game Design Elements in Non-Game Contexts*. ACM.
13. Gerling, K. M., & Masuch, M. (2011, May). Exploring the potential of gamification among frail elderly persons. In *Proceedings of the CHI 2011 Workshop Gamification: Using Game Design Elements in Non-Game Contexts*. ACM.
14. Ryan, R. M., & Deci, E. L. (2000). Self-determination theory and the facilitation of intrinsic motivation, social development, and well-being. *American Psychologist, 55*(1), 68–78.
15. McGonigal, J. (2011). *Reality is broken: Why games make us better and how they can change the world*. New York: Penguin Press.
16. Reeves, B., & Read, J. L. (2009). *Total engagement: Using games and virtual worlds to change the way people work and businesses compete*. Boston: Harvard Business Press.
17. Ryan, R. M., Rigby, C. S., & Przybylski, A. (2006). The motivational pull of video games: A self-determination theory approach. *Motivation and Emotion, 30*(4), 344–360.
18. Csíkszentmihályi, M. (2008). *Flow: The psychology of optimal experience*. New York: Harper Perennial Modern Classics.
19. Deci, E. L., & Ryan, R. M. (2000). The "what" and "why" of goal pursuits: Human needs and the self-determination of behavior. *Psychological Inquiry, 11*(4), 227–268.
20. Pink, D. H. (2010). *Drive: The surprising truth about what motivates us*. Edinburgh: Canongate.

21. Huotari, Kai & Hamari, Juho (2011, May). Gamification from the perspective of service marketing. In *Proceedings of the CHI 2011 Workshop Gamification: Using Game Design Elements in Non-Game Contexts*. ACM.
22. Oliver, R. L. (1993). A conceptual model of service quality and service satisfaction: Compatible goals, different concepts. *Advances in Services Marketing and Management, 2*, 65–85.
23. Spreng, R. A., & Mackoy, R. D. (1996). An empirical examination of a model of perceived service quality and satisfaction. *Journal of retailing, 72*(2), 201–214.
24. Rollings, A., & Adams, E. (2003). *Andrew rollings and ernest adams on game design*. Indianapolis: New Riders Games.
25. Shneiderman, B. (2004). Designing for fun: how can we design user interfaces to be more fun? *Interactions, 11*(5), 48–50.
26. Saito, A. (2008). Gamenics and its potential. In K. Isbister & N. Schaffer (Eds.), *Game usability: Advancing the player*. San Francisco: Morgan Kaufmann.
27. Norman, D. A. (2004). *Emotional design: Why we love (or hate) everyday things*. New York: Basic Books.
28. Lazzaro, M. (2008). The four fun key. In K. Isbister & N. Schaffer (Eds.), *Game usability: Advancing the player*. San Francisco: Morgan Kaufmann.
29. Lepper, M., & Malone, T. (1987). Intrinsic motivation and instructional effectives in computer based education. Snow.
30. Bialoskorski, L. S. S., Westerink, J. H. D. M., & van den Broek, E. L. (2010). Experiencing affective interactive art. *International Journal of Arts and Technology, 3*(4), 341–356.
31. Sauer, J., & Sonderegger, A. (2010). The influence of product aesthetics and user state in usability testing. *Behaviour & Information Technology*.
32. González Sánchez, J. L., Gutiérrez Vela, F. L., Montero Simarro, F., & Padilla-Zea, N. (2012). Playability: analysing user experience in video games. *Behaviour & Information Technology, 31*(10), 1033–1054.

Chapter 10
BaLOReS: A Framework for Quantitative User Interface Evaluation

Salvador González López, Francisco Montero Simarro, and Pascual González López

Abstract Nowadays, graphical user interfaces (GUI) are expected to be more than mere shop windows for their applications. In fact, if the users' interactive expectations are not reasonably satisfied by the GUI, any functional capability of the software may be ignored. In order to improve satisfaction through aesthetically well-designed interfaces, we present a suite of five structural principles known as BaLOReS, together with five aesthetic metrics. These principles help designers to structure their mockups which are later assessed through the metrics. A complementary prototyping tool, BGLayout, has also been provided to automate the calculation of these measurements. Finally, a full case study is given to illustrate how to use the proposed tool to apply these metrics to an entire interface.

10.1 Introduction

A GUI is the part of a software which allows or hinders or quite simply highlights the advantages or disadvantages users find in an application. A user interface (UI) has not only the capability but also the responsibility of transmitting the product's virtues to users through a satisfactory interaction which answers their needs.

Human-computer interaction (HCI) studies the use of software by analyzing all interaction aspects, whether related with design, user comprehension, information architecture, etc. HCI proposes a wide variety of actions applicable during the design stage focused on improving user experience and in its highest form gives rise to the philosophy of user-centered design or UCD, which aims to involve users in the entire software life cycle in order to improve the quality and performance

S. González López (✉) • F. Montero Simarro • P. González López
LoUISE Research Group, Computer System Department, University of Castilla-La Mancha,
Avda. España s/n, 02071, Albacete, Spain
e-mail: salvador.gonzalez2@alu.uclm.es; fmontero@dsi.uclm.es; pgonzalez@dsi.uclm.es

V.M.R. Penichet et al. (eds.), *New Trends in Interaction, Virtual Reality and Modeling,*
Human-Computer Interaction Series, DOI 10.1007/978-1-4471-5445-7_10,
© Springer-Verlag London 2013

[1–3]. Since the 1990s, the proliferation of development frameworks has facilitated the emergence of thousands of disposable applications which do not follow any specific methodology and have low-quality interfaces.

In order to provide a tool for software development, international standards have proposed quality models at different levels: for process (ISO/IEC 12207:2008), evaluation (ISO 15504:2008), and product (ISO 9241-11:1998, ISO/IEC 9126-1:2001, ISO/IEC 9126-3:2003). All of them are undoubtedly useful for achieving quality software products, and they have spread well-known terms like *friendly interface, interface with a high degree of usability*, or *interface with a high level of quality in use*. The usability metrics proposed by these organizations usually focus on semantic or procedural aspects of the interaction and do not cover the quality parameters related to aesthetics. In this work, we keep treating the need for aesthetic principles and metrics that help designers to generate better interface mockups and propose a suite of design principles together with their metrics under the name of BaLOReS [4]. We have also developed an interface prototyping tool (BGLayout) to automatically calculate the metrics and to indicate any parts of a design with low scores that need to be improved.

This chapter has been organized as follows: Section 10.2 reviews related works to identify the main design principles. Section 10.3 discusses these principles and justifies the selection of a minimal set, which are described in Sect. 10.4 together with examples. In Sect. 10.5, the five structural metrics are detailed and calculated for simple interfaces, and another equation is proposed for the composition of the results returned by the metrics. In Sect. 10.6, a complete case study is described showing how the metrics can be recursively applied to evaluating more complex designs. Section 10.7 presents some conclusions and describes future work.

10.2   Design Metrics and Principles

As it is now generally recognized that interface usability is an important part of the overall quality of any software, many researchers have highlighted the need for using predictive metrics during the interface design phase in order to improve final usability [5, 9, 18].

In 1994, the *Interface Metric Project* was an important initiative which provided a suite of predictive metrics oriented towards improving the design process. The aim of the project was to propose early application metrics, easy to calculate, conceptually solid, and related to broadly accepted principles of good design. As a result of this work, the *Essential Usability Metric Suite* [2] was proposed, composed of five metrics that offer designers information on the degree of usability of their interfaces. These metrics are as follows: *essential efficiency, task concordance, task visibility, layout uniformity*, and *visual coherence*. The first three are procedural, task related, and based on essential use cases. The fourth, *layout uniformity* (LU), is structural and serves to assess the interface layout. This metric, as we will see later, has certain shortcomings whose resolution will be part of the germ of our proposal.

The last one, *visual coherence*, checks the coherence of the design with regard to the meaning of widgets. Apart from the first, these metrics are all percentages, in which 100 % represents full compliance with the factor and 0 % is absolute noncompliance. Further information on the metrics can be found in [2].

The relation between aesthetics and usability is well known, and it has already been shown how aesthetics determines the perceived usability [10–12]. As it has been proved that certain visual pleasing properties can positively motivate the use of a software [2], the present proposal aims to improve the interface through the composition of its widgets. However, unsatisfactory composition may achieve the opposite effect.

In spite of the subjectivity of aesthetic aspects, several authors have characterized user interfaces according to certain design principles [2, 3, 10, 13]. In this work, we considered the set of principles collected by Wilbert O. Galitz in [3] as a starting point, as they are generally acceptable concepts of visually pleasing design. They are, in short, the principles of *balance*, *symmetry*, *regularity*, *economy*, *predictability*, *sequentiality*, *unity*, *proportion*, *simplicity*, and *grouping*. A detailed analysis of these principles, while outside the scope of this work, determines that aesthetically pleasing composition goes beyond visual parameters and that these simple properties are often difficult to assess. In the following section, these criteria are discussed and more meaningful ones are selected to form the minimal suite of principles.

10.3 Looking for a Set of Minimal Principles

A set of measurable principles that sum up the best qualities of good design should be selected in order of priority. *Structural* or *semantic* principles could be the first; if the principle is based on aesthetic aspects (widgets alignment, number of different dimensions, or formatting), it should be classified as structural. If it is based on semantic aspects (design consistency, chance of use, or relative importance), it should be classified as semantic. The classifications can be seen in Table 10.1.

As our interest lay in studying how aesthetic characteristics can improve interface usability, we opted to consider five strictly structural principles: balance, symmetry, regularity, sequentiality, and proportion. Structural principles are often easier to measure on interfaces than those based on semantic parameters, and they can be checked in the early mockups of the interface. The first step was to consider these five structural principles in the light of the questions: *Is it possible to aesthetically*

Table 10.1 Principle classification according to its nature

	Balance	Symm.	Regular.	Econo.	Predict.	Sequent.	Unity	Proport.	Simplic.	Group.
Semantic	–	–	–	✓	✓	–	✓	–	✓	✓
Structural	✓	✓	✓	✓	✓	✓	✓	✓	✓	✓

Table 10.2 Application, usage, and benefits of treated principles

	Application	Actual use	Benefit
Balance	*Layouting, form design, menus*	*High*	*High*
Symmetry	*Layouting*	*Low*	*Low*
Regularity	*Layouting, regular menus, tables*	*High*	*High*
Sequentiality	*Layouting, several kinds of menus, lists of elements*	*High*	*High*
Proportion	*Images' dimensions*	*Low*	*Medium*

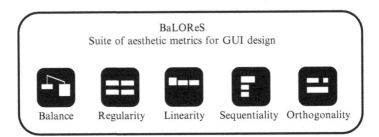

Fig. 10.1 BaLOReS: suite of aesthetic metrics

characterize any interface with these principles? Are all of them really relevant? To answer these questions, we observed the actual use of each principle and checked their cost against possible benefits. Our impressions are summed up in Table 10.2.

According to the collected information, only three of the five principles proved to be of interest (*balance*, *regularity*, and *sequentiality*) and thus form the heart of our suite.

The principle of symmetry, although important in the field of art, was not included because of its low relevance to interface design. Indeed, the principles of balance and regularity are quite similar to symmetry and can cover most cases, so we decided to leave out symmetry due to the absence of any rules for its application.

At this stage, we had a set of three relevant principles to assess interface design; however, we were aware that this set could not of itself characterize a wide range of designs, so we completed the suite with two more principles which somehow complemented the others. According to the literature, the principle of sequentiality is the provision of vertically aligned elements on the interface, so we included the analog principle of *linearity,* understood as the provision of horizontally aligned elements, which is present in linear designs such as menu bars. We also saw the need to add another principle to check the vertical and horizontal alignment of non-regular elements. This principle was given the name of *orthogonality* and is a generalization of the principle of regularity. In the end, we came up with a five-principle suite that we think can be applied to the vast majority of interfaces, composed of the principles of balance, linearity, orthogonality, regularity, and sequentiality, which together form the acronym BaLOReS. The icon for each principle (see Fig. 10.1) reflects the kind of design each aims to achieve. These principles are explained in detail in Sect. 10.4, together with several applications.

Fig. 10.2 Case of balanced interface (www.dropbox.com)

10.4   BaLOReS: A Suite of Aesthetic Principles for User Interfaces

The BaLOReS suite aims to be a predictive tool that estimates the degree of usability of prototypes and interfaces, the early stages of design, and also final user interfaces. Each of the principles is described below.

10.4.1   Balance

Balance gives the suite one of its most interesting features by providing the notion of equilibrium or the equal weight of two areas on either side of a line. The balance does not need to be totally symmetrical nor does it imply the same dimensions for both regions. It may be of interest in distributing areas in a layout or in creating forms. An example can be seen in Fig. 10.2. The balance icon shown in Fig. 10.1 represents the adjustment of visual equilibrium, and this notation can be used in a layout design to denote the presence of this aesthetic principle.

10.4.2   Linearity

In reading and writing, human beings prioritize horizontal provisions (left to right) over vertical ones (top to bottom). This is why it is common in interface design

Fig. 10.3 Example of
interface with linearity
(*Vine app*)

Fig. 10.4 Example of
sequentiality (*Gmail app
for iOS*)

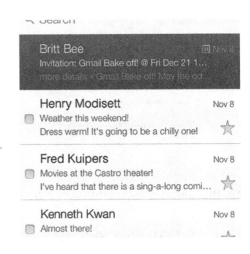

to organize closely related horizontal sets of components that should be read as a
line. The principle of linearity occurs when elements are horizontally aligned, for
instance, in menu bars, distribution of panels, or rows. The linearity icon shown in
Fig. 10.1 indicates the horizontal alignment of elements. These elements are not
necessarily identical and could be aligned at the top, bottom, or center. Figure 10.3
shows an example of this principle.

10.4.3   Sequentiality

The vertically analogous term to linearity is sequentiality, which is used to distribute
graphic elements from the top downwards. From a visual point of view, sequentiality
has a weaker group sense than linearity, due to our way of reading. The icon for
this principle can be seen in Fig. 10.1. Sequentiality can be achieved by aligning
UI elements along a vertical line, either on the left, right, or center. This way of
organizing a space is quite frequent in many user interfaces, in layouts, forms, lateral
menus, or long item lists (see Fig. 10.4).

Invisible Children

Mission #4: Ask your head of state to support the international effort to bring an end to LRA violence and rehabilitate the affected region. Need inspiration? See examples here: http://bit.ly/HD5zaH Over and out.

Ver traducción

Cover The Night Mission #4: Contact Your Heads of State
www.youtube.com

For more details visit: http://www.kony2012.com/ For questions on how to participate email: ctn@invisiblechildren.com For Kit Download and Int'l Resources Vis...

Me gusta · Comentar · Compartir · 👍703 💬135 📋122 · Hace aproximadamente una hora · ↩

Fig. 10.5 Orthogonal layout in www.facebook.com

10.4.4 Orthogonality

Orthogonality represents the degree of vertical and horizontal alignment, i.e., the degree of perpendicularity of a design. We consider this principle as the least orthodox of BaLOReS since it fits in with many kinds of two-dimensional design. The icon shown in Fig. 10.1 for this principle shows a typically simple orthogonal layout. Unlike regularity, orthogonality allows differently shaped elements to be organized in incomplete rows or columns. This non-regular way of organizing has interesting properties, it gives the design good readability thanks to the rows, and the design is orderly, similar to comic boxes. Orthogonality can be seen as a combination of linearity and sequentiality, achieving designs which combine both visual layouts. In practice, it is useful for ordering items vertically or horizontally (see Fig. 10.5). It is important to note that some interfaces contain more than one design principle. Later, we will explain how to assess interfaces with several design criteria.

10.4.5 Regularity

Regularity is similar to orthogonality, since both are used to organize two-dimensional elements in the interface. However, regularity implies the identical shape and size of items. Regularity is achieved by harmonizing an element's dimensions and spacing among the rows and columns. Mesh-form is reached in highly regular designs. This principle was included for its high frequency and its ability to arrange items in such a way as to give them visual equality (see icon in Fig. 10.1). However, if some elements are bigger than others, the design highlights them. A highly regular interface can be seen in Fig. 10.6.

Fig. 10.6 Example of regular
design (*Flipboard app*)

At this point, five important aesthetic principles have been described. The vast
majority of interfaces could be designed using this set of rules. To complete our
framework, five respective metrics are given to evaluate them.

10.5 BaLOReS: A Suite of Aesthetic Metrics for Graphical User Interfaces

Our proposal was born from considering other suites of metrics on interface
aesthetics. International standards for software products, such as ISO/IEC 9126-
3:2003, as well as tools like MUSiC and DRUM tend to assess usability by
performance or functional metrics, which often need mature interfaces to apply
them [14, 15]. Nevertheless, we felt there was a need for designers to be helped
with the layout from the beginning of the design process, so we opted to apply
our set of metrics to both low-fidelity prototypes and also finished interfaces.
The *Essential Usability Metric Suite* [2] is one of the best known. These metrics,
although they may improve interface usability, only assess the visual design through
layout uniformity or *LU*. The fact that a design should be evaluated simply by
LU goes against the idea that design is above all creative and heterogeneous. We
therefore decided to look for different aesthetic criteria to better characterize the
nature of different interfaces. In fact, it is by no means unusual to find cases in
which layout uniformity scores low in visually appealing designs (see Fig. 10.7).

In spite of being scored from 0 % to 100 %, the authors of layout uniformity
explain that good designs score between 50 % and 85 % [2]. This is because scores
under 50 % are not regular, and those close to 100 % may have too much gridding,
which is not frequent in UI design. This could lead to uncertainty and gives rise
to the questions: *how to choose the right design from several designs which score*

Google
Google Search
I'm Feeling Lucky
Make a silent movie by talking to Chrome

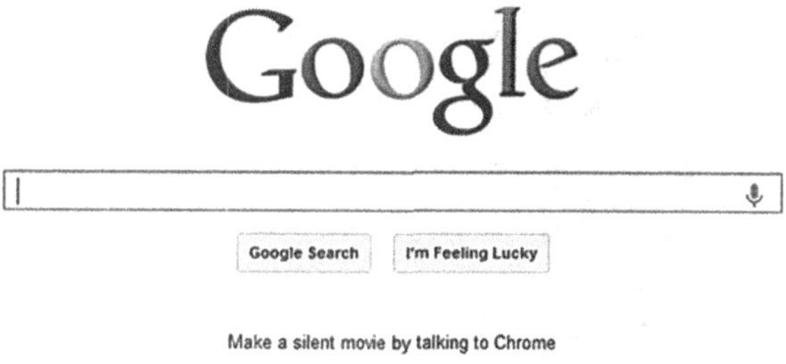

Fig. 10.7 Bad design interface according to LU = 22 % (www.google.com)

Cómo empezar a utilizar Gmail
Nombre:
Apellido:
Nombre de registro:
@gmail.com
Ejemplos: ARamos, Ana.Ramos
Comprobar disponibilidad
Cómo empezar a utilizar Gmail
Nombre:
Apellido:
Nombre de registro:
@gmail.com
Ejemplos: ARamos, Ana.Ramos
Comprobar disponibilidad

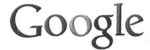

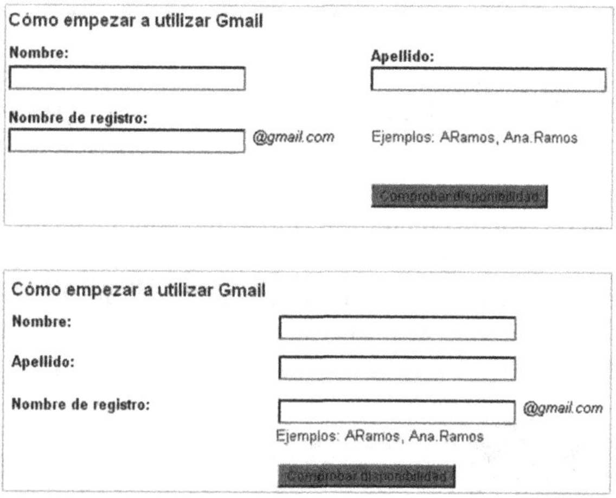

Fig. 10.8 63% and 55 % LU designs, respectively

between 50 % and 85 %? How can LU be used to select design alternatives? (see Fig. 10.8). Based on our experience, layout uniformity may therefore not be a reliable tool for the designer.

Unlike other proposed metrics, we wanted ours to be dynamic and scalable. As interfaces are highly heterogeneous, a dynamic evaluation process adaptable to different interactions is critical. Interfaces are also scalable as they contain successive nesting layers, so we included a composition expression to combine isolated results into a single global result.

BaLOReS consists of five specific metrics focused on the five selected principles of balance, linearity, sequentiality, orthogonality, and regularity. Each of these interface areas or panels can be checked with whatever metric the designer wishes. This suite therefore does not specify the use of one metric for each panel in the interface, meaning that some areas may be left unevaluated. In spite of this, the framework is able to provide an overall score on the interface composition, which is one of the most important points in our proposal. The suite was designed so that every metric would return values from 0 to 1. 0 means the absence of the measured principle, and 1 total fulfillment. The acceptability level is therefore established at approximately 0.5.

Fig. 10.9 Interface where Ba = 0.75 (www.youtube.com)

10.5.1 Balance

The balance metric (Ba) is inspired by the concept of an equilibrium between two areas separated by a vertical line, achieved by giving similar visual weight to both sides. Since the quantification of this weight is subjective, it was decided to make a heuristic that considers weight as the accumulated height of the components on each side. This was experimentally verified, and the final expression is as follows (Eq. 10.1):

$$Ba = \frac{n_{hac}}{n_c}\left(1 - \frac{|h_l - h_r|}{h_l + h_r}\right) \tag{10.1}$$

where:

n_{hac} = number of components horizontally aligned with other components
n_c = number of components in the interface
h_l = accumulated height of left side components
h_r = accumulated height of right side components

Another aspect considered in this metric is the left-right association through row design in order to maintain a certain relationship between the information on both sides.

Figure 10.9 illustrates the use of this metric in a panel from YouTube. In this case, there is not only good balance but also a good relationship between image and text. The metric outcome is 0.75, which indicates an acceptable balance (values over 0.5 are acceptable).

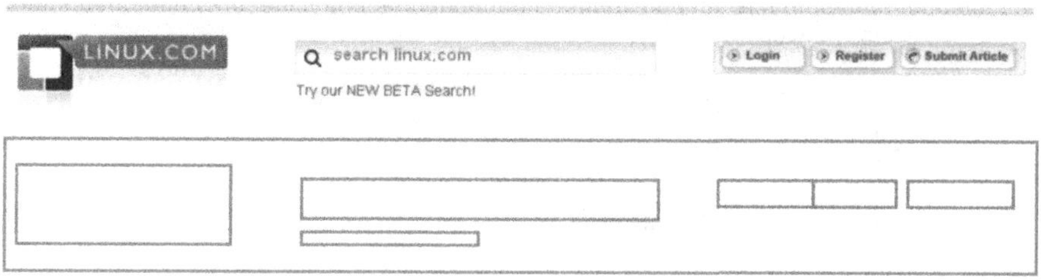

Fig. 10.10   Interface with Li = 0.83 (www.linux.com)

10.5.2   Linearity

As already mentioned, linearity should measure the horizontally aligned arrange-
ment of the element in the interface. Equation 10.2 shows the linearity metric (Li).
As can be seen in Fig. 10.10, there is a high degree of linearity with only one vertical
alignment. The metric score is 0.83, a sufficiently high value that denotes good
horizontality in this design.

$$Li = \frac{n_{hac} \times n_{va}}{n_c{}^2} \qquad (10.2)$$

where:

n_{hac} = number of components horizontally aligned with other components
n_{va} = number of different vertical alignments
n_c = number of components in the interface

10.5.3   Sequentiality

Sequentiality is the vertically analogous metric to linearity, so its approach and
mathematical expression are quite similar:

$$Se = \frac{n_{vac} \times n_{ha}}{n_c{}^2} \qquad (10.3)$$

where:

n_{vac} = number of components vertically aligned with other components
n_{ha} = number of different horizontal alignments
n_c = number of components in the interface

Fig. 10.11 Interface where Se = 0.66 (www.coches.net)

Sequentiality is intended to arrange every design component vertically without interfering with the horizontal organization, as in Fig. 10.11, in which the metric returned a value of 0.66 for sequentiality (Se).

10.5.4 Orthogonality

Orthogonality considers the perpendicular alignment of elements of different shapes and sizes, i.e., it ensures that every component is horizontally and vertically aligned.
This dynamic metric has important advantages:

- It does not require a specific type of design.
- It allows a vast number of different designs with multiple elements.
- It combines elements in many different ways.
- It covers designs that other metrics do not cover.

The expression of this metric (Or) is shown below (Eq. 10.4).

$$Or = \frac{n_{vac} \times n_{hac}}{n_c{}^2} \tag{10.4}$$

where:

n_{vac} = number of components vertically aligned with other components
n_{hac} = number of components horizontally aligned with other components
n_c = number of components in the interface

In spite of the disparity of the elements in Fig. 10.12, the metric gave a value of 0.75, which indicates a reasonably orthogonal design. At this point, the designer must decide on the level of his quality requirements.

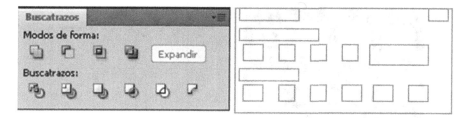

Fig. 10.12 Panel with Or = 0.75 (*Adobe Illustrator CS5*)

10.5.5   Regularity

The suite also includes a metric for regularity (Re) (see Eq. 10.5):

$$Re = \frac{n_{vac} \times n_{hac} \times (n_c - n_s + 1)}{n_c{}^3} \tag{10.5}$$

where:

n_{vac} = number of components vertically aligned with other components
n_{hac} = number of components horizontally aligned with other components
n_c = number of components in the interface
n_s = number of different shapes

   Comparing this metric with orthogonality, it is easy to see that regularity is a particular case of orthogonality with the addition of a third factor, which means the higher the number of elements with the same shape, the better the result. Figure 10.13 shows a case of uniform modular design. This type of design is highly rated by our metric at a value of 1.

10.6   Composition of Metrics

If the first feature of BaLOReS is its capability to assess aesthetically designs, the second is the capacity of composing isolated values given by several metrics of the suite in one global value. It is possible because metrics have been designed to be applicable to selective areas in the interface as designer wishes. Thus, once calculated the metric for each group of elements, a composition expression is given to generate a global score representative of whole interface. This particular feature was not found in any other suite of metric studied in the bibliography. Equation 10.6 shows the expression for composition in terms of the interface's inner areas.

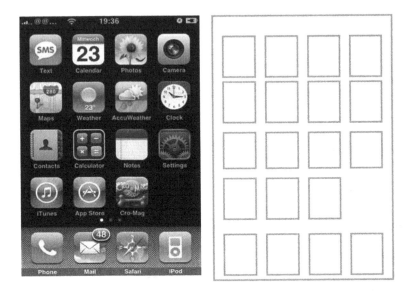

Fig. 10.13 Case with Re = 1 (*iOS menu*)

$$Composition = \frac{a_{p_1} \times m_{p_1} + \ldots + a_{p_i} \times m_{p_i}}{a_{p_1} + \ldots + a_{p_i}} \tag{10.6}$$

where:

p_i = nonempty panel or area with metric defined
a_{p_j} = panel area expressed in pixel^2
m_{p_i} = calculated metric in p_i panel

Analyzing this expression, it can be seen that each of the regions which has a set metric contributes according to the size of its area, so that the suite is sensitive to the relative importance of each panel in relation to the whole interface.

Although BaLOReS was created with the intention of covering any type of design, situations were also considered in which it is impossible to find an appropriate metric for a certain area. In these cases, it is possible to leave the interface without an assessment without influencing the composition. Figure 10.14 shows how to carry out the overall process. Abstracting the interface layout, it is easy to see that it is subdivided into three subpanels. The process is simply to establish a metric for each panel and then calculating the metric. The results can be joined to the composition expression to get an overall result of 0.72. This overall value indicates that according to the aesthetic principles considered, in this case orthogonality, sequentiality, and linearity, the interface has been composed satisfactorily.

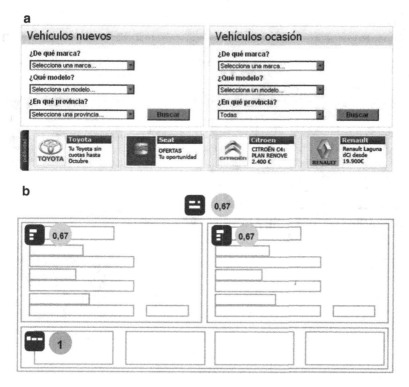

Fig. 10.14 Capture from www.coches.net (**a**) and corresponding assessed prototype (**b**)

10.7 BGLayout

To calculate this and the other metrics dealt with in this paper, a graphic tool was developed that can load screen captures or create interface prototypes from scratch to assess their composition. This tool, developed from a previous one [16, 17], is known as BGLayout and can be downloaded free at http://bglayout.tk.

The process of assessing an interface from a capture is quite simple. First, it is necessary to create a new *Screen* clicking in the toolbar and select the option "Yes, I have a template" in the dialog to choose an image file. The option "No, I'll do from zero" will be selected only to begin with an empty prototype. Once the image has been selected, it is necessary to delimit the elements of the interface adding new *Screen-Area*. After that, screen-areas have to be assessed with metrics according to their designs, and based on these intermediate values calculate the composition metric. These features can be reached in the menu *Tools > Metrics*. In Fig. 10.15, the *Flipboard* interface is evaluated and overlaid results are displayed. In the upper-left corners of each container area, results are shown in white; however, overall value is located in the lower-right corner in green.

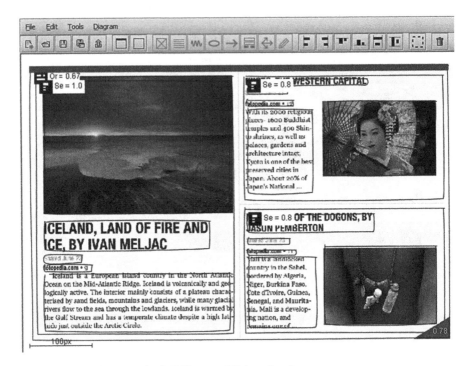

Fig. 10.15 Interface assessing in BGLayout (*Flipboard app*)

10.8 Conclusions

User interface design combines different knowledge areas and the skills of design, interaction, psychology, and development, among others. HCI puts them in order by providing the tools to achieve better designs and more user-friendly systems. We believe the proposed suite of principles and metrics to be a step in this direction, as it provides a framework for aesthetic interface composition.

To create this framework, a set of structurally oriented and highly adaptive minimal aesthetic principles was first defined. The five principles of balance, linearity, orthogonality, regularity, and sequentiality together form the acronym BaLOReS. These principles were then quantified by the metrics for appropriate evaluation. The metrics were deliberately designed to be easily calculated simply with a pen and paper. This framework is also complemented by a software tool, BGLayout, to facilitate the calculations.

The set of metrics proposed here have only been validated empirically, so that a further deeper statistical study is needed, which is already being carried out. We are also working on the automatic calculation of these metrics from screen captures with BGLayout and the help of pattern-recognition techniques. Finally, we wish to make it clear that although the metrics proposed here are quantitatively oriented, we want to emphasize the fact that the designer's judgment should always prevail over these measurements, since the real intention of BaLOReS is to provide him with a tool for reflecting on and improving his designs. Neither is it our intention to provide automatic UI generation, but rather a framework for producing more appealing interfaces.

Acknowledgments The described activities are partially funded by the following projects: PEII09-0054-9581, TIN2008-06596-C02-01 y TIN2012-34003.

References

1. Abras, C., Maloney-Krichmar, D., & Preece, J. (2004). User-Centered Design. In W. Bainbridge (Ed.), *Encyclopedia of human-computer interaction*. Thousand Oaks: Sage Publications.
2. Constantine, L. L., & Lockwood, L. A. D. (1999). *Software for use: A practical guide to the models and methods of usage-centred design*. New York: Addison-Wesley.
3. Galitz, W. O. (2007). *The essential guide to user interface design an introduction to GUI design principles and techniques* (3rd ed., pp. 8–145). New York: Wiley.
4. González, S., Montero, F., & González, P. (2012). BaLOReS: A suite of principles and metrics for graphical user interface evaluation. In *Proceedings of 13th International Conference on Interación Persona-Ordenador* (Art No. 9). Elche: Spain.
5. Bassat, T. B., Meyer, J., & Tractinsky, N. (2006). Economic and subjective measures of the perceived value of aesthetics and usability. *ACM Transactions on Computer-Human Interaction, 13*(2), 210–234.
6. Lok, S., Feiner, S., & Ngai, G. (2004). Evaluation of visual balance for automated layout. In *Proceedings of International Conference of Intelligent User Interaction '04* (pp. 101–108). Madeira: Portugal.
7. Mugge, R., & Schoormans, J. P. L. (2012). Product design and apparent usability. The influence of novelty in product appearance. *Applied Ergonomics, 43*, 1081–1088.
8. Sauro, J., & Kindlund, E. (2005). A method to standardize usability metrics into a single score. In *Proceedings of the SIGCHI '05* (pp. 401–409). Portland: Oregon, USA.
9. Sears, A. (1993). Layout appropriateness: A metric for evaluating user interface widget layouts. *IEEE Transactions on Software Engineering, 19*(7), 707–719.
10. Ngo, D. C. L. (2001). Measuring the aesthetic elements of screen designs. *Displays, 22*, 73–78.
11. Purchase, H. C., Hamer, J., Jamieson, A., & Ryan, O. (2011). Investigating objective measures of web page aesthetics and usability. In *Proceedings of 12th Australian User Interface Conference*. Perth: Australia.
12. Sonderegger, A., & Sauer, J. (2009). The influence of design aesthetics in usability testing: Effect on user performance and perceived usability. *Applied Ergonomics, 41*, 403–410.
13. Vanderdonckt, J., & Gillo, X. (1994). Visual techniques for traditional and multimedia layouts. In *Proceedings of Advanced Visual Interfaces '94* (pp. 95–104). Bari: Italy.
14. Macleod, M., Bowden, R., Bevan, N., & Curson, I. (1997). The MUSiC performance method. *Behaviour and Information Technology, 16*, 279–293.
15. Sears, A. (1995). AIDE: A step toward metric-based interface development tools. In *Proceedings of the ACM Symposium on User Interface Software and Technology* (pp. 101–110). Pittsburg: Pensilvania, USA.
16. Blankenhorn, K. (2004). A UML profile for GUI layout. Master Thesis, Department of Digital Media, University of Applied Sciences, Furtwangen.
17. Montero, F., & López, V. (2010). GUILayout++: Supporting prototype creation and quality evaluation for abstract user interface generation. In *Proceedings of 1st Workshop on UsiXML* (pp. 39–44). Berlin: Germany.
18. Comber, T., & Maltby, J. R. (1997). Layout complexity: Does it measure usability?. In *Proceedings of INTERACT '97* (pp. 623–626). Sydney: Australia.

Printed in the United States
By Bookmasters